WITHDRAWN

THE GOLDEN
CONSTANT

THE GOLDEN CONSTANT

THE ENGLISH AND AMERICAN EXPERIENCE
1560–1976

ROY W. JASTRAM

University of California, Berkeley

A RONALD PRESS PUBLICATION

JOHN WILEY & SONS, New York • Chichester • Brisbane • Toronto

Library of Congress Cataloging in Publication Data

Jastram, Roy W   1915–
  The golden constant.

  "A Ronald Press publication."
  Includes index.
  1. Gold—History. 2. Prices—United States—
History. 3. Prices—Great Britain—History.
I. Title.

HG289.J33   332.4′222′0941   77-15034
ISBN 0-471-02303-5

Printed in the United States of America

10 9 8 7 6 5 4 3 2 1

To my wife Virginia

As much hers as it is mine

Preface

My interest in gold began in 1936 for a pragmatic reason. As the most junior member of the Stanford University Department of Economics, I was chosen to volunteer to do some research commissioned by Mr. C. O. G. Miller, an industrialist and gentleman scholar. Through his readings in history, Mr. Miller had become interested in the basic question: Was money worth more in past centuries than it is today?

I chose gold as the monetary medium most likely to admit of consistent definition over time, so the design of the study became a statistical analysis of the purchasing power of gold for as many centuries as I could find reliable data. The modest paper that resulted became the personal property of Mr. Miller and was never published.

I thought I was through with the subject, but the interest aroused by the research stayed with me; so over the years I read intermittently and without conscious plan whatever new materials relating to gold came to hand.

Then the explosion of gold prices in 1968 fixed my

attention. Could we better understand what was going on in the present if we knew more about the historical relationship of gold to other prices? Might we find something systematic in its history to give us a more perceptive appreciation of current monetary events? Would it be useful to others to enlarge my earlier work? My enforced interest of 1936 became the inception of the present volume.

In preparation and writing I have had help from a number of individuals and sources I wish to acknowledge here. In England I benefited from talks with Mr. A. T. Bell of the Bank of England, Mr. Peter Fells, Consolidated Gold Fields, Limited, and Mr. Robert Guy, Director of N. M. Rothschild and Sons, who presides over the daily gold price fixing by the five principal bullion dealers in London and has a deep sense of history.

Invaluable aid came from the staffs of the following libraries: The Research Library, Bank of England; The Goldsmiths Library, University of London; The Guildhall Library, London; The University of California Library, Berkeley; The Stanford University Library; and The Kress Library, Harvard University.

Professor J. K. Galbraith generously loaned me his staff to explore the resources of the Harvard libraries.

I wish it were possible to thank certain unidentifiable individuals at the British Museum who allowed me to track down some obscure sources in ways that were clearly unorthodox for that venerable institution.

Financial support for the research activity came from the Institute of Business and Economic Research of the University of California, Berkeley.

Mr. Timothy Green, the author of *The World of Gold Today*, has my appreciation for turning over to me data compiled for future volumes of his own.

I value the encouragement given me by Professor A. H. John, Professor of Economic History at the London School of Economics. To a greater extent than he realizes, the gracious reception he gave me and the numerous conversations we shared contributed to the pleasure of writing this book.

In the United States I wish to acknowledge informative discussions with Professors Robert A. Gordon, Carlo M. Cipolla, John M. Letiche, and Austin C. Hoggatt of my own faculty.

I was aided greatly in data collection and technical analysis by my two excellent research assistants, Dr. Aharon Hibshoosh and Mr. Christopher Miller. Peter Blatman was of great help in the computer-related portions of the study. Ms. Patricia Murphy oversaw the processing of the manuscript and its appendages with commendable skill and good humor.

Professor Edward S. Shaw of Stanford University read the entire manuscript with his usual care and perception and made valuable suggestions.

Obviously, these people who tried to be helpful should not be blamed for any imperfections in the book.

ROY W. JASTRAM

Carmel Valley, California
June 1977

Contents

Tables and Charts

THE GOLDEN CONSTANT

INTRODUCTION

This book is essentially a quantitative study in the economic history of England and the United States. The time frame is 1560–1976.

The quantitative method was chosen to transpose speculative thought into actual numbers. Able scholars and inquisitive laymen have conjectured for centuries about the economic role of gold and the causes of its fluctuations in value and purchasing power. My aim is to crystallize these speculations by the use of quantitative evidence, and in so doing to provide a useful perspective on the past, an improved understanding of the present, and, possibly, clues to the future. I shall be especially alert for any recurring themes—any constancies—in the last four centuries of the history of gold.

It is, therefore, as a statistician that I approach this excursion into economic history; I do not presume to take on the role of an economic historian or a monetary economist as well. But, as is evident to anyone examining the tables and charts presented, major historical events did occur simultaneously with major changes in the price and purchasing power of gold. These events must be noted in any approach to an understanding of the history of gold. In this book these episodes are described, and their relevance to my immediate subject is suggested. It remains for the economic historian and the monetary theorist to explore their causal significance fully.

Two separate streams of statistics run through the course of this study. One deals with the general behavior of commodity prices over long periods of time; the other, moving concurrently, deals with the price of a single commodity—that commodity is gold.

Why gold? Why is gold selected from all other commodities for this purpose? It is not my intent to add to the voluminous literature on the pervasiveness of gold in most cultures, its uses in art, religion, metaphysics, or even as a source of power. I select gold for a thoroughly pragmatic reason. Let me explain. . . .

Traditionally, in economics, our standard of value for comparative purposes in different times, places, and contexts is human effort. How many hours did a stone mason have to work on the cathedral at Canterbury to feed his family for the day? How long must a mason now work on a new office building in Manchester for the same purpose? This is standard methodology.

But many kinds of wealth or earnings cannot be represented by man-hours. It makes no sense to conceive of the quarterly earnings of the Bank of America, say, in man-hour equivalence, let alone that institution's total assets. Much the same irrelevance holds for an individual's financial holdings or earnings on personal investments. There is, however, one common way the value of all forms of assets, fixed or liquid, and all kinds of income, earned or otherwise, can be evaluated. That common denominator is a precious metal, usually gold.

Note that I am not saying that gold is a *better* measure of value than human effort; it is an alternative measure and often is more fitting to the circumstances of a particular comparison.

Having chosen gold as the standard of comparison, and its purchasing power as the subject for analysis, let me propose another idea: that of *operational wealth*.

Operational wealth is a new term but not a new concept. It describes the ability of a person to "operate" with his dollars. This ability depends on two factors: (a) the number of dollars he has, and (b) the prices of things he might want to command with them. For example, his monetary wealth may remain constant at $100,000, but his operational wealth will be cut in half if prices double or will double if prices are halved.

Operational wealth is really a convenient fiction, because our measure can include fixed or liquid assets, or both, since it speaks of the dollar equivalence *if* the right to employ them to command other things at going prices is exercized.*

The schema of the work is as follows:

- To construct a unified series of the price of gold since 1560 utilizing market prices, Bank of England buying prices, and Mint prices.

- To construct a unified series representing the level of wholesale commodity prices in every year since 1560.

- To determine the statistical relationship between the first two series in such a way as to measure the purchasing power of gold (operational wealth) since 1560.

- To discover the behavior of the purchasing power of gold in periods of inflation and deflation.

- To judge the extent to which gold has served as an infla-

---

*Operational wealth has a close counterpart in economic jargon in "real wealth," which in turn is analogous to "real income." These latter terms were coined by the classical economists of the nineteenth century to describe what money income alone would buy. I use neither since the opportunities for confusion are too great for those readers who may consider gold to be the only *real* wealth, in contrast to paper money.

tionary hedge in history and a conservator of operational wealth in periods of price recession.

Our *conceptual* scheme, then, is (a) to convert monetary wealth into operational wealth to reflect purchasing power, and (b) to express operational wealth in terms of gold equivalence to have comparability at all times and places.

Our corresponding *analytical* scheme is to take the price of an ounce of gold over time and adjust it for changes in the prices of other goods—in short, to measure the purchasing power of gold as shown in Table 3.

England is the principal but not the only geographic setting for this examination of economic history. There are several reasons for this choice, some obvious and some not so apparent.

England is a country for which data are available over unusually long spans of time. She represents an economy with constant *political* boundaries for many centuries. (Germany, Italy, and France, not unified until much later, underwent shifts in boundaries until modern times.) England has not been invaded by a foreign power since 1066. She has supported and suffered many wars, but this is not the same as being occupied by foreign troops and subjected to the levies and disruptions thereby created.

England has had a remarkably consistent monetary table over time. From the Norman Conquest until the change to decimal coinage in 1971, English money has consisted of pounds, shillings, and pence, always with 20 shillings to the pound and 12 pence to the shilling. For about 700 years there was no break between the money of one year and the next. The coinage and the money of account never parted company. In all other European countries the price historian must, at some time, translate one denomination into another and decide whether to translate at the rate of exchange decreed by authority or by the rate recognized in the marketplace.

Most significant of all, England represents an economy that has been at the heart of economic development and global

transactions for many generations. Although the English economy itself has never been large in a demographic sense, it has
for centuries been the center of financial and commercial transactions and the paths of trade. The economy of all the Western
world, and much of the Eastern, has impinged on England.
Economic decisions and activities originating in England have
affected the rest of that world for all the decades covered by the
present volume.

My final reason for choosing to use England is that the English
are a nation of record keepers. From the time they learned to
cipher they kept accounts of everything that interested them.
And three things that did interest them enormously were trade,
money, and prices.

This combination of longevity of consistent records, constant
boundaries and monetary system, unoccupied soil, and economic importance cannot be found in any other country. England is a paragon for statistical analysis of an historical character.

The chief source of commodity prices in England is the
monumental work done by Lord Beveridge and his associates,
published as *Prices and Wages in England from the Twelfth to the
Nineteenth Century*, Vol. I, 1939. I cannot commend too highly
this remarkable achievement. A prodigious effort went into its
compilation, and a reader of the original is bound to be impressed by the meticulous care exercized to secure validity. It
contains prices for nearly 170 commodities and is more completely discussed when its material is used in Chapter 3.

Why does this history begin with 1560? For a single reason—it
was the year of the Great Recoinage. Until then English coinage
had been for years in a chronically doubtful state. Debasement
and defacement became particularly severe after 1540. By the
death of Henry VIII in 1547, purchasing power had depre-
ciated by roughly 20 percent. This decline continued precipitously so that by 1560 the pound would probably buy about
one-half the commodities it commanded two decades earlier. It
was then that Queen Elizabeth set out "to achieve to the victory

and conquest of this hideous monster of the base money"
(Dyson's *Proclamations,* 35).

It is part of the lore of money that Sir Thomas Gresham did at
this time formulate and pronounce to the Council of State his
"law" that bad money drives out good and thus persuaded a
vacillating government to replace wholesale, base coins with new
issues. However instrumental Gresham was, he is hardly likely to
have accomplished the trick with an epigram. Astute as we know
him to be, he probably did not try it at all in that informed
company.

The proposition goes back at least as far as Aristophanes
(Macaulay, *History,* Vol. IV, p. 623n) and was long known in
England, as evidenced by petitions addressed to the Parliaments
of Edward III and Richard II hundreds of years earlier.

The Great Recoinage of 1560 was not the last of England's
troubles with base currency and light coins. But it was a major
reform toward a currency for meaningful price comparisons
over time and, therefore, gives a useful starting point for this
book.

Matching the English experience topic by topic, I have also
analyzed the relevant data for the United States that was, after
all, an English colony until the late eighteenth century. The
period runs from 1800 to the present time, a relatively short
period compared to England. This country does not, of course,
match all the historical attributes cited earlier for the choice of
England, but thorough attention to it is fully justified by its great
importance both as a national economy and as an economic
influence on the rest of the world. Further, a study of gold in the
United States is a logical companion piece to the study of England, because economic institutions are common to the two and
similar motivations and traditions influence their commerce and
finance.

PART ONE
THE ENGLISH EXPERIENCE

1   The Price of Gold

Gold is not a self-limiting subject. Any discussion of gold requires delineation to keep it manageable.

This is a study of the ability of a precious metal to command other goods in exchange for itself. It is not a treatise on money as such. Yet the role of gold as a basis for currency is so imbedded in economic history that it is well to sketch briefly the monetary role of gold as background for this statistical study of its purchasing power.

THE PENNY AND THE POUND

The history of the English pound starts with the history of the English penny. The earliest form of the latter word is "pending" and is thought to come from silver coins issued by King Penda, who established the power of Mercia in the first half of the seventh century. In the next hundred years these coins spread throughout the Saxon kingdoms and were exchanged by count (or "tale"), with 240 of them always being called a "pound."

A statute of 1266 decreed that the penny should weigh "thirty-two wheat corns in the midst of the ear," and there are suggestions that this enactment simply made official an old tradition. A later statute of 1280 stated that the penny should weigh 24 grains, which by the schedule of weights official at that time was as much as the former 32 grains of wheat. Thus the 24-grain pennyweight came into being and was continued into the sixteenth century, when troy weight began to be used in the Mint.*

Early in the twelfth century the penny was called a "sterling," a designation that probably comes from "steorra," meaning star, because some of the early pennies were so imprinted. These coins gained a wide reputation on the Continent for their consistent fineness, and the term of approbation, "sterling silver," grew out of their ready acceptance and the respect accorded them. Ultimately, the designation became current for the pound sterling. But this reputation of the English pound was built on the quality of the silver penny, rather than the other way around.

THE CHANGING ROLE OF GOLD AND SILVER

Before the close of the seventeenth century silver was the effective basis for English coinage and hence for the common flow of everyday transactions. Gold coins first strayed into England in the course of international trade. As the export trade in tin,

---

*William the Conqueror had set up his principal Mint in the Tower of London. At that time he adopted what he named the "Tower pound," which later proved to be 6.25 percent lighter than the troy pound. This is an important matter of terminology, because early records sometimes read in one system, sometimes the other.

hides, and wool grew after the Conquest, the gold coins of Byzantium, known as "besants" and widely circulated in Europe, entered England in large quantities.

In 1257 Henry III minted the first English gold penny of 45 troy grains which he proclaimed current for 20 pence. This gold penny failed because there was little use for it in the England of that time. In large transactions it failed because at 20 pence it was undervalued in terms of silver. In small transactions it was too high a denomination for convenience.

Starting with the gold penny of 1257, fourteen different English gold coins were issued by 1717. Gold coinage was no stranger to early England, but it never caught on with the public until the eighteenth century was well under way.

Because of its high value in relation to the income of most people, gold could not handle the common business of the communities as well as silver. However, as time went on the nature of dealings and the size of individual transactions were gradually moving toward magnitudes that made gold coins convenient and, therefore, acceptable. Wages still could not be paid in gold, but an increasing proportion of production was passing into the control of capitalists who could use gold in their typical size of transactions with merchants and the larger agriculturists.

One major factor that began to accelerate the proportionate substitution of gold for silver was the rising volume of trade with the East, thanks largely to the activity of the East India Company. Much to the chagrin of the English wool industry, the people of India simply were not interested in exchanging their merchandise for the good, warm cloth of England. But they loved silver. In one year alone, 1717, the East India Company exported three million ounces of silver, much of which we must assume came from melting down English silver coins.

Along with this outflow of silver was an influx of gold, for quite a different reason. The resumption of peace with France in 1713 increased tremendously England's trade with that nation, and the French settled their trade balances in gold. Therefore, what was occurring in England was a major shift in the internal stocks of gold and silver. Gold was flowing in as silver was flowing out. Gold was no longer undervalued in terms of silver, and this was reflected in the narrowing ratio of gold to silver prices. In addition, silver coins were melted down and disappearing, and gold coinage was taking their place. During the 3 years following peace in 1713 over 4 million pounds' worth of gold was minted. England, without plan, conscious motivation, or perhaps general realization, was rapidly moving toward a de facto gold standard.

THE GOLD STANDARD COMES TO ENGLAND

Important to the understanding of this section is the history of guinea coins. As so often is the case in English history, nobody named it; that is what it came to be called because the tiny imprint of an elephant showed that the gold came from Africa. The warrant for the issue of this gold coin was dated Christmas Eve 1663. Its nominal face value was 20 shillings.

The guinea never did go for exactly 20 shillings. As early as January 1665 we know that it went for 21 shillings 4 pence in actual circulation. It appears to have always been well above 21 shillings until the event we are about to describe.

Since the gold guinea was passing in the streets at higher than its face value in terms of the silver shilling, clearly the ratio of the face value of the two coins was out of line with the price ratio existing in the bullion markets. As so often is the case, the government tried to solve this economic impasse by edict. A proclamation was issued on December 22, 1717 forbidding any person to give or receive guineas at a *higher* price than 21 shillings (and reducing any other gold coins in due proportion).

As Master of the Mint, Sir Isaac Newton (yes, the same one) wrote a brilliant report on the imbalance. But even he did not foresee fully the consequences of the disequilibrium. A passage from Sir Isaac Newton's report helps to make clear what happened:

> If things be let alone till silver money be a little scarcer the gold will fall of itself. For people are already backward to give silver for gold and will in time refuse to make payments in silver without a premium as they do in Spain and this premium will be an abatement in the value of gold. And so the question is whether gold shall be lowered by the Government of let alone till it falls of itself by the want of silver money.

In other words, Newton realized that the two metals could not continue to circulate side by side in coined form at the existing ratio between the bullions. If they were both to remain in circulation, either gold must come down or silver go up. What he did not seem to realize was the portentous difference between the two alternatives.

The odd thing, therefore, is that England did not establish the gold standard by any design or deliberate act. The proclamation of December 22, 1717 brought the golden guinea down to 21 shillings. If guineas, by the ordinary working of supply and demand, had then come down to less than 21 shillings and shilling pieces (the silver coin) continued to pass for 12 pence, the currency would still have been based on a silver standard. But if guineas remained at 21 shillings and the shilling pieces went to a premium, then ipso facto England had changed over to a gold standard. The guinea stood fast. The value of 21 shillings in money was tied to the value of *gold* in a guinea and not to the value of *silver* in 21 shilling pieces.

It was a classic case of "Let the marketplace decide."

The foregoing is a matter of monetary history. One reason for recounting it here is to dispose of the idea that the purchasing power of gold was of no importance before England went officially on the gold standard at a much later time. The relation was not solemnized until 1816 following the Napoleonic Wars, with Lord Liverpool's Act establishing gold as the sole standard.

But a full century earlier one of the great currencies of all time had quietly eased onto the gold standard at a Mint price of 3 pounds, 17 shillings, 10.5 pence (£3.17s. 10.5d) per standard ounce.

THE PHILOSOPHY OF HARD MONEY

This is a time to tell of the origin among the English of a high regard for sound money.

In the 1690s the coinage was in one of its chronic states of disarray. John Locke, best known to us as a philosopher, was called in by Somers, the Lord Keeper, to give his views. Locke was in frequent association with Sir Isaac Newton, who seems to have agreed with him on this occasion, but only the views of Locke come down to us in his essay entitled *Further Considerations Concerning Raising the Value of Money*.

The heart of this is preshadowed in the Dedication of the book to Lord Keeper Somers:

> Westminster Hall is so great a witness to your Lordship's unbiased justice and steady care to preserve to everyone their right, that the world will not wonder you should not be for such a lessening our coin as will, without any reason, deprive great numbers of blameless men of a fifth part of their estates beyond the relief of chancery.

Locke advanced, thereupon, the argument of the injustice to the creditors that would result if the bullion content of the unit of account were reduced. The only true pound, he maintained, was 3 ounces, 17 pennyweight 10 grains of sterling silver, and the only justice that could be done was by recoining all the money at this previous rate.

Locke's view prevailed over the opposition of the goldsmiths, the bankers, and many commercial men. For the first time since 1299 a recoinage was made (1697–1698) that restored completely the standard which prevailed before the debasement.

The sanctity that Locke attached to the Mint weights was something new. (It is significant that is took a philosopher to do it.) Before his essay surely very few people had regarded the weights of coins in any way as immutable. Kings had made coins. They had altered them many times, and surely if they cared to do so they would alter them again. As early as the fifteenth century the notion that the Mint weights should not be changed had disappeared entirely. Coinage was regarded as a prerogative of the King, who might do with it as he pleased.

After 1696, however, the gospel according to Locke persisted. Peel, in 1819 and again in 1844, stood firmly on Locke's doctrine that the pound was a definite quantity of bullion that must not be altered. Thus the prominent writers of the nineteenth century praised the settlement of 1819 by which the old standard was restored. Mainly as a lengthened shadow of Locke, 3 pounds, 17 shillings, 10.5 pence an ounce came to be regarded as a magic price for gold from which England ought never to stray and to which, if she did, she must always return as soon as possible.

THE STATISTICS OF GOLD PRICES

There are three ways that English gold prices are presented in historical records:

1. Market prices
2. Bank of England buying prices
3. Mint prices

Market prices mean prices arrived at between freely acting individuals or institutions as terms for the exchange of bullion for unrestricted usage. Bank of England buying prices are those at which the Bank stands ready to receive gold, whether or not actual exchange takes place. On any given day the Bank may not have any takers. But if it had posted for that day a price which it would pay, that was the buying price. Mint prices, similarly, are prices at which the Mints stand ready to buy.

These three prices are not necessarily the same. For much of the period 1870–1914, for example, the Mint prices stood at 3 pounds, 17 shillings, 10.5 pence, whereas the Bank of England bought at 3 pounds, 17 shillings, 9 pence per standard ounce. In fact the Bank was legally obligated under the Act of 1844 to buy any gold offered at 3 pounds, 17 shillings, 9 pence and to pay its notes in sovereigns, which was the equivalent of selling gold at 3 pounds, 17 shillings, 10.5 pence. It could raise the buying price if it wished, but it could not go below the floor of 3 pounds, 17 shillings, 9 pence.

During this time (1870–1914) the average annual *market* price in London fluctuated within the limits of 3 pounds, 17 shillings, 9 pence and 3 pounds, 17 shillings, 11.23 pence (Shrigley, p. 92). The latter was touched once in 1897, which was a very unusual year. With almost the entire world on or preparing to go on the gold standard there was much competition for gold. Focusing on this same period, 1870–1914, we see only one other year (1893) when the London market price averaged higher than the Mint price at 3 pounds, 17 shillings, 10.57 pence.

In other words, over this particularly significant period for the world's treatment of gold the London *market* price nearly always fluctuated within the limits of the Bank's buying price on the one hand and the Mint price on the other. And even in 1897 the market price became less than one-fourth of one percent above the Bank's *minimum* buying rate. The average premium of market price over the Bank's minimum buying price was only 0.057093 percent for the entire 45 years culminating in 1914 (gold seems to attract decimal points).

It is important to recognize the nature of these three prices and the narrow relationship among them, for we sometimes have to deal with one and at other times with another.

A WORLD ON THE GOLD STANDARD: A DIGRESSION

The years just noted (1870–1914) were the period in the world during which gold was most widely esteemed as a monetized metal. London dominated the financial sphere as never before or since. Most of the important nations, by reasons of commerce or industry, followed England onto the gold standard. Germany, Holland, and the Scandinavian countries did so early in the 1870s, with Switzerland, Belgium, and France doing so all in the one year of 1878. Austria followed in 1892, Japan in 1897, Russia in 1899, and Italy in 1900. Indian mints halted receipt of silver, and in 1899 the British sovereign (gold) was made legal tender. The more sizable countries of South America shifted their standards to gold early in the twentieth century. The only important country remaining on the silver standard was China.

Following the Civil War the United States used inconvertible paper until 1879, when it resumed specie payment on a de facto monometallic gold standard. The gold standard was formalized in 1900 with the Gold Standard Act of that year (see p. 140). Lloyd George could later say about this time, "The crackle of a bill on London was as good as the ring of gold in any port throughout the civilized world."

With more nostalgia than complete accuracy, the English gold standard in the three decades preceding World War I often is represented as smooth, automatic, and as nearly perfect an institution as can be devised for disparate peoples to deal with one another.

Actually, the English monetary system, with the Bank of England at its center, did not match up to this ideal. The gold standard was never the perfect machine for untended economic evenhandedness that a somewhat romantic view would impute to it.

To repeat my remarks at the opening of this chapter, gold is not a self-limiting subject, and now I must end this digression, which is not wholly immaterial to the statistics of the price of gold. However, the reader whose curiosity needs satisfaction may look at Sir Albert Feavearyear's *The Pound Sterling,* Chapter XII, "Sterling and the International Gold Standard."

THE STATISTICS OF GOLD PRICES AGAIN

There are the three prices with which we have to deal historically. My preference is for the market price, whenever that can be ascertained. This is mainly from a sense of symmetry. We subsequently discuss the purchase of commodities at open market prices, so it seems fitting to compare the price of gold on the open market. Sometimes, when both the Bank and Mint prices are artificially restricted, the open market price may be the only realistic one to use.

There is a certain trade-off in this choice. The Mint price can be ascertained as far back as 1343, so it has the advantage of longevity and continuity. I was able to find open market price series of substantial length only for 1760–1829 and from 1870 to the present, hence these have less continuity but more economic significance. The Bank buying price is available to fill in where needed, and I use it between 1829 and 1870.

My preference is in this order: (a) market prices, (b) Bank buying prices, and (c) Mint prices; and I select accordingly in constructing a unified series showing fluctuations in the price of gold since 1560. For my purpose it is the *proportionate* changes over time that count.

Because of the liquidity and mobility of gold, these price series probably do not get very far apart except under artificially constrictive conditions. The close sympathy between market prices and Bank buying prices was illustrated before for the period 1870–1914, with the average difference between the two less than 0.06 percent.

The main objective in the statistical construct of a single unified series is to splice one kind of series to another so that no
spurious leap or decline is caused when a switch is made from
one type of quotation to another fluctuating at a higher or lower
level. This is easily done and is explained at the appropriate
time. Let me simply lay out the schema now:

1560

       Dependent on Mint prices

1716

1717

       Dependent on Bank buying prices

1759

1760

       Dependent on London market prices

1829

1830

       Dependent on Bank buying prices

1869

1870

       Dependent on London market prices

1976

The Goldsmiths Library in London has scattered issues of *The
Course of the Exchange*, a twice-weekly sheet put out first by a
broker named John Castaing and continued by various brokers
thereafter. On a frequent, but somewhat irregular, basis these
contain market prices of gold in bars from 1719 to 1746. The
earliest quotations are 3 pounds, 17 shillings, 9 pence. Later
quotations of 3 pounds, 17 shillings, 11 pence appear frequently. These quotations are not given with sufficient regu-
larity for index number construction, but they do verify that the
use of Bank buying prices from 1717 through 1759 is well in line
with market prices for much of the period.

The Bank buying price and the open market price are linked in another transactional way over substantial periods of history. Either the goldsmiths (bullion brokers) bought on behalf of the Bank or certainly kept the Bank informed of market prices.

In testimony before "The Select Committee appointed to inquire in the Cause of the High Price of Gold Bullion" (the Bullion Committee) in 1810, we have some enlightening remarks from Aaron Asher Goldsmid, Esq., partner in the "House of Mocatta and Goldsmid, Bullion Brokers." Mocatta and Goldsmid had been founded 226 years earlier in 1684 (10 years before the Bank of England) and still flourishes today.

QUESTION: Can you state what tables (of gold prices) are most perfect in your Judgment?

ANSWER: Those published by Wettenhall are likely to be correct; they are made from our reports to the person who furnishes him with the prices.

QUESTION: Is the price derived by Wettenhall from the information of others, or only from your reports to him?

ANSWER: From ours alone.

QUESTION: Are those prices always real prices taken from actual transactions, or are they ever nominal?

ANSWER: Always the real prices.

*   *   *

QUESTION: Have you not frequently transactions both of purchase and sale with individuals, in which the Bank is not concerned?

ANSWER: There are many transactions in which the Bank is not concerned; but they are all inserted in a book in the Bullion Office. (earlier) Such information can be procured from the books of the Bullion Office in the Bank; *all of our sales are through the medium of that Office* (italics added).

QUESTION: For what reason are they so inserted?

ANSWER: I believe that they have been so since the establish-
            ment of the Bank (1694).

QUESTION: Was it in order that the bank might be apprised of
            the transactions, and regulate their proceedings ac-
            cordingly?

ANSWER: Possibly.

QUESTION: State in detail the mode in which such a transaction
            is made with an individual.

ANSWER: The Bullion is received from one individual and
            delivered to another at the price fixed by us; and
            the whole of the transaction is recorded in the
            books of the Bullion Office in the Bank, with the
            names of the parties, the amount sold, and the
            price.

QUESTION: Is not every quantity of bar gold which by your
            intervention passes from one individual to another,
            deposited for some time in the Bank, and assayed
            there?

ANSWER: Yes.

QUESTION: Have you not, in certain cases, bought and sold gold
            without the intervention of the Bullion Office in
            the Bank at all?

ANSWER: None.

                        *   *   *

QUESTION: Have you not, in certain cases, bought and sold gold
            been confined to individuals, or has the Bank been
            a purchaser?

ANSWER: Individuals have been the purchasers of large
            quantities of gold at the present high price. (The

reader should note that this was the period of the Napoleonic Wars.)

QUESTION: Are there any other Brokers in the same line besides your house?

ANSWER: Our house has been solely employed since the year 1694, at the establishment of the Bank.

QUESTION: Are there any other dealers in gold but yours?

ANSWER: I apprehend none of considerable amount.

QUESTION: Are there others recorded in the Bullion Office in the Bank like yours?

ANSWER: None.

If we put this all together, we see that the firm of Mocatta and Goldsmid was by far the largest bullion broker in England, that it dealt on private account as well as for the Bank of England, that it informed the Bank routinely of the price of every private transaction, and that this arrangement had been in place since the Bank's founding in 1694.

This highly interactive arrangement was further pinned down 9 years later when another member of the firm, Mr. Issac Lyon Goldsmid, was testifying before "The Secret Committee on Expediency of the Bank Resuming Cash Payments."

QUESTION: What is your line of Business?

ANSWER: I am a Partner in the House of Mocatta and Goldsmid, who are Brokers between the Bank and Merchants, and between Merchants and Merchants, in Bullion.

QUESTION: How long have you been so?

ANSWER: Twenty years as a Partner and seven years as a Clerk. The House had been Brokers to the Bank ever since it was established.

* * *

QUESTION: In making purchases of Bullion for the Bank, or
             for Merchants, is it possible for the Seller to learn
             whether you are purchasing for an Individual or
             for the Bank?

ANSWER: He is not generally informed of it. When there is an
             arrival of Bullion, a Communication takes place
             between the Seller and ourselves, either by our
             applying to him, or by our being sent for; we give
             him all the information we possess concerning the
             State of the Market and he forms his own Opinion
             with reference to the Exchanges, or with respect to
             any other Circumstances, at what Price he will sell.
             Supposing the Bargain to be completed, having
             discovered a Purchaser, we send him a Contract of
             Sale, and he delivers the Bullion at the Bullion
             Office of the Bank, whether it is purchased on
             account of the Bank or of a Merchant, and he
             receives Payment in Bank Notes. The Clerk of the
             Bullion Office does not part with the Bullion, un-
             less the Purchaser pays for it at the same Moment. I
             should have mentioned, that we send early on the
             following Morning the Particulars of the Transac-
             tion to the Clerk at the Bullion Office, the Names of
             the Seller and of the Purchaser, the Quantity and
             the Price. If the Bank are the Purchasers or Sellers,
             they have the Names of the Buyer or the Seller; if
             other Persons buy or sell, the Names are generally
             not given either of the Buyer or the Seller, as we
             are oftend enjoined to Secrecy, as the Knowledge of
             the Parties would frequently counteract subsequent
             Operations. The Clerk of the Bank is acquainted
             with all Particulars.

So we see that there were not two independent markets, one

for dealings with the Bank of England and another for dealings between two private parties in the open. The common link between the two markets is the bullion broker. One would, therefore, expect close interdependence between the two prices.

This is a further reason for my order of preference of (a) the market price, (b) the Bank's buying price, and (c) the Mint price. The first two are closely linked through the historic arrangement of the bullion market. (N. M. Rothschild & Sons, Ltd., was founded as the London branch of the family operation in 1804, and by the crisis of 1825 had become bullion broker for the Bank. During the near depletion of reserves in that crisis, Rothschilds were instructed to buy gold wherever it could be found, and it brought in several million pounds within a few days. It was buying at even higher than the Mint price—a rare occasion indeed.)

In constructing the unified price series from 1560 to 1976 for this study, the market price is used first, the Bank buying price second, and the Mint price only when the other two are lacking.

THE TYING TOGETHER OF THE UNIFIED SERIES: THE INDEX OF GOLD PRICES

I cannot discover a market price from any one source consistently earlier than 1760. And I have the Bank buying price only as far back as 1717 (coincidentally, the year the gold standard became effective). Earlier than that the old standby, the Mint price, is the one available.

In the year of overlap, 1717, the Mint price stood at 3 pounds, 17 shillings, 10.5 pence and the Bank buying price at 3 pounds, 17 shillings, 6 pence. The Mint price was, therefore, spliced in to the level of the existing Bank price by the appropriate ratio of reduction. Then going back in time every Mint price was multiplied by the ratio 77 shillings, 6 pence/77 shillings, 10.5 pence until 1560, the beginning year of the entire study.

At this stage we have from 1560 through 1759 either the actual Bank buying price or an approximation to it via an adjusted Mint price. From 1760 through 1829 we have an exceptional collection of London market prices compiled by Mr. John White, Cashier of the Bank of the United States, in November 1829. By taking a year of overlap with the Bank buying price in 1760, these market prices are spliced in to extend the unified series from 1560 through 1829.

From 1829 through 1869 I again rely on the buying price of the Bank of England. Then from 1870 to the present we have reliable market prices based on London from several well-recognized sources. All these separate series are given in the Appendix D.

With the unified series spliced together in shillings as described, we are now ready to put them on an index number basis so that the *proportional* fluctuations in the price of gold can be portrayed over the last four centuries (and so that they can later readily be compared with proportional fluctuations in commodity prices).

The index of gold prices is constructed by expressing the price of gold in each year for the entire series as a percentage of the price of gold in 1930. The base year of 1930 was selected because it is the last before the onset of continuous gold price gyrations beginning in 1931, and it was preceded by almost constant prices since 1925. The results would have been statistically identical if I had set 1925–1930 average = 100.0.

Tables 1, 2, and 3 are basic to the English experience, and are presented here together for continued and easy reference. Chart I depicts the data in the three tables for the period 1560–1976.

The derivation of the statistics on gold prices given in Table 1 is explained in Appendix D. The computation of the commodity price index presented in Table 2 is the subject of Chapter 3. The data on the purchasing power of gold in Table 3 are fully discussed in Chapter 4.

Table 1

THE INDEX OF THE PRICE OF GOLD

England 1560–1976

$(1930 = 100.0)$

Year	Index	Year	Index	Year	Index
1560	69.8	1591	69.5	1622	84.9
1561	69.8	1592	69.5	1623	84.9
1562	69.8	1593	69.5	1624	84.9
1563	69.8	1594	69.5	1625	84.9
1564	69.8	1595	69.5	1626	84.9
1565	69.8	1596	69.5	1627	84.9
1566	69.8	1597	69.5	1628	84.9
1567	69.8	1598	69.5	1629	84.9
1568	69.8	1599	69.5		
1569	69.8			1630	84.9
		1600	69.5	1631	84.9
1570	69.8	1601	70.3	1632	84.9
1571	69.8	1602	70.3	1633	84.9
1572	69.8	1603	70.3	1634	84.9
1573	69.8	1604	76.0	1635	84.9
1574	69.8	1605	76.0	1636	84.9
1575	69.8	1606	76.0	1637	84.9
1576	69.8	1607	76.0	1638	84.9
1577	69.8	1608	76.0	1639	84.9
1578	69.8	1609	76.0		
1579	69.8			1640	84.9
		1610	76.0	1641	84.9
1580	69.8	1611	82.3	1642	84.9
1581	69.8	1612	84.3	1643	84.9
1582	69.8	1613	84.3	1644	84.9
1583	69.8	1614	84.3	1645	84.9
1584	69.8	1615	84.3	1646	84.9
1585	69.8	1616	84.3	1647	84.9
1586	69.8	1617	84.3	1648	84.9
1587	69.8	1618	84.3	1649	84.9
1588	69.8	1619	84.9		
1589	69.8			1650	84.9
		1620	84.9	1651	84.9
1590	69.5	1621	84.9	1652	84.9

Table 1 (Continued)

Year	Index	Year	Index	Year	Index
1653	84.9	1690	94.7	1727	99.5
1654	84.9	1691	94.7	1728	99.5
1655	84.9	1692	94.7	1729	99.5
1656	84.9	1693	94.7		
1657	84.9	1694	94.7	1730	99.5
1658	84.9	1695	94.7	1731	99.5
1659	84.9	1696	104.2	1732	99.5
		1697	104.2	1733	99.5
1660	84.9	1698	104.2	1734	99.5
1661	84.9	1699	101.8	1735	99.5
1662	84.9			1736	99.5
1663	94.7	1700	101.8	1737	99.5
1664	94.7	1701	101.8	1738	99.5
1665	94.7	1702	101.8	1739	99.5
1666	94.7	1703	101.8		
1667	94.7	1704	101.8	1740	99.5
1668	94.7	1705	101.8	1741	99.5
1669	94.7	1706	101.8	1742	99.5
		1707	101.8	1743	99.5
1670	94.7	1708	101.8	1744	99.5
1671	94.7	1709	101.8	1745	99.5
1672	94.7			1746	99.5
1673	94.7	1710	101.8	1747	99.5
1674	94.7	1711	101.8	1748	99.5
1675	94.7	1712	101.8	1749	99.5
1676	94.7	1713	101.8		
1677	94.7	1714	101.8	1750	99.5
1678	94.7	1715	101.8	1751	99.5
1679	94.7	1716	101.8	1752	99.5
		1717	99.5	1753	99.5
1680	94.7	1718	99.5	1754	99.5
1681	94.7	1719	99.5	1755	99.5
1682	94.7			1756	99.5
1683	94.7	1720	99.5	1757	99.5
1684	94.7	1721	99.5	1758	99.5
1685	94.7	1722	99.5	1759	99.5
1686	94.7	1723	99.5		
1687	94.7	1724	99.5	1760	101.4
1688	94.7	1725	99.5	1761	102.7
1689	94.7	1726	99.5	1762	102.5

Table 1 (Continued)

Year	Index	Year	Index	Year	Index
1763	103.3	1800	109.1	1837	99.8
1764	101.4	1801	110.4	1838	99.8
1765	100.1	1802	106.5	1839	99.8
1766	101.6	1803	102.7		
1767	102.2	1804	102.7	1840	99.8
1768	102.0	1805	102.7	1841	99.8
1769	103.0	1806	102.7	1842	99.8
		1807	102.7	1843	99.8
1770	103.1	1808	102.7	1844	99.8
1771	102.4	1809	116.4	1845	99.8
1772	102.7			1946	99.8
1773	100.0	1810	118.1	1847	99.8
1774	99.5	1811	128.4	1848	99.8
1775	99.6	1812	138.6	1849	99.8
1776	99.6	1813	138.6		
1777	99.6	1814	141.2	1850	99.8
1778	99.6	1815	134.8	1851	99.8
1779	99.5	1816	102.7	1852	99.8
		1817	100.7	1853	99.8
1780	99.5	1818	104.6	1854	99.8
1781	99.5	1819	104.0	1855	99.8
1782	99.8			1856	99.8
1783	98.8	1820	100.0	1857	99.8
1784	100.0	1821	100.0	1858	99.8
1785	100.0	1822	99.4	1859	99.8
1786	99.5	1823	99.4		
1787	99.5	1824	99.4	1860	99.8
1788	99.5	1825	99.8	1861	99.8
1789	99.5	1826	99.4	1862	99.8
		1827	99.4	1863	99.8
1790	99.5	1828	99.4	1864	99.8
1791	99.5	1829	99.8	1865	99.8
1792	99.5			1866	99.8
1793	99.5	1830	99.8	1867	99.8
1794	99.5	1831	99.8	1868	99.8
1795	99.5	1832	99.8	1869	99.8
1796	99.5	1833	99.8		
1797		1834	99.8	1870	99.8
1798	100.0	1835	99.8	1871	99.8
1799	99.8	1836	99.8	1872	99.8

Table 1 (Continued)

Year	Index	Year	Index	Year	Index
1873	99.8	1908	99.9	1942	220.7
1874	99.8	1909	99.9	1943	220.7
1875	99.8			1944	220.7
1876	99.8	1910	99.9	1945	220.7
1877	99.8	1911	99.9	1946	220.7
1878	99.8	1912	99.9	1947	220.7
1879	99.8	1913	99.9	1948	220.7
		1914	99.9	1949	220.7
1880	99.8	1915	99.9		
1881	99.8	1916	99.9	1950	319.1
1882	99.8	1917	99.9	1951	319.1
1883	99.8	1918	99.9	1952	319.1
1884	99.8	1919	106.0	1953	319.1
1885	99.8			1954	319.1
1866	99.8	1920	132.9	1955	319.1
1887	99.8	1921	125.9	1956	319.1
1888	99.8	1922	109.8	1957	319.1
1889	99.8	1923	106.2	1958	319.1
		1924	110.2	1959	319.1
1890	99.8	1925	99.3		
1891	99.9	1926	99.9	1960	319.8
1892	99.9	1927	99.9	1961	319.1
1893	99.9	1928	99.9	1962	319.1
1894	99.8	1929	99.9	1963	319.1
1895	99.8			1964	319.1
1896	99.9	1930	100.0	1965	319.1
1897	100.0	1931	108.8	1966	319.1
1898	99.9	1932	138.9	1967	319.1
1899	99.8	1933	146.9	1968	418.7
		1934	161.9	1969	420.4
1900	99.9	1935	167.2		
1901	99.8	1936	165.1	1970	378.8
1902	99.9	1937	165.6	1971	405.2
1903	99.8	1938	167.6	1972	623.0
1904	99.9	1939	182.4	1973	1038.8
1905	99.8			1974	1660.0
1906	99.9	1940	220.7	1975	1863.7
1907	99.9	1941	220.7	1976	1697.5
				. . .	. . . .

Table 2

THE INDEX OF WHOLESALE COMMODITY PRICES

England 1560–1976

(1930 = 100.0)

Year	Index	Year	Index	Year	Index
1560	40.0	1591	57.7	1622	66.3
1561	42.6	1592	59.6	1623	63.5
1562	25.7	1593	60.6	1624	64.9
1563	39.9	1594	62.6	1625	65.4
1564	32.0	1595	51.1	1626	66.0
1565	41.1	1596	55.0	1627	69.8
1566	48.7	1597	54.7	1628	72.2
1567	49.6	1598	53.6	1629	69.9
1568	49.6	1599	55.9		
1569	48.4			1630	70.9
		1600	55.7	1631	72.5
1570	48.1	1601	56.2	1632	72.0
1571	49.2	1602	63.1	1633	71.9
1572	46.5	1603	57.2	1634	74.1
1573	49.0	1604	57.2	1635	74.2
1574	48.1	1605	60.3	1636	74.0
1575	45.1	1606	61.7	1637	76.1
1576	45.5	1607	63.3	1638	73.7
1577	45.0	1608	64.1	1639	73.4
1578	44.2	1609	62.4		
1579	44.5			1640	77.4
		1610	63.1	1641	89.1
1580	45.9	1611	65.2	1642	78.0
1581	45.7	1612	65.5	1643	74.2
1582	45.8	1613	66.2	1644	75.0
1583	49.9	1614	68.6	1645	76.4
1584	48.3	1615	67.4	1646	80.0
1585	48.7	1616	66.6	1647	89.0
1586	57.0	1617	67.0	1648	88.1
1587	56.8	1618	68.2	1649	91.9
1588	57.5	1619	65.7		
1589	57.7			1650	87.0
		1620	65.8	1651	86.8
1590	57.6	1621	66.1	1652	92.4

Table 2 (Continued)

Year	Index	Year	Index	Year	Index
1653	86.9	1690	86.8	1727	92.7
1654	85.9	1691	82.8	1728	92.7
1655	87.7	1692	88.5	1729	87.7
1656	90.6	1693	88.7		
1657	92.1	1694	91.1	1730	89.3
1658	96.0	1695	93.7	1731	89.3
1659	85.2	1696	88.1	1732	85.1
		1697	86.4	1733	81.4
1660	80.7	1698	88.3	1734	81.0
1661	83.3	1699	86.9	1735	83.9
1662	80.2			1736	80.1
1663	82.3	1700	82.7	1737	79.9
1664	82.4	1701	85.5	1738	80.3
1665	87.1	1702	81.1	1739	86.0
1666	84.5	1703	82.3		
1667	82.0	1704	85.8	1740	100.1
1668	78.1	1705	86.9	1741	98.4
1669	75.7	1706	85.6	1742	92.5
		1707	86.6	1743	90.8
1670	77.9	1708	89.3	1744	91.8
1671	77.4	1709	92.2	1745	94.3
1672	79.4			1746	104.6
1673	80.8	1710	98.5	1747	94.6
1674	79.9	1711	94.6	1748	95.3
1675	73.9	1712	97.4	1749	85.9
1676	78.8	1713	97.6		
1677	79.5	1714	98.4	1750	88.3
1678	74.7	1715	97.5	1751	87.7
1679	79.6	1716	98.1	1752	83.2
		1717	96.4	1753	85.1
1680	80.6	1718	96.4	1754	87.9
1681	81.7	1719	103.2	1755	89.1
1682	81.5			1756	91.7
1683	82.6	1720	86.0	1757	91.8
1684	86.1	1721	91.8	1758	92.3
1685	83.7	1722	90.9	1759	91.7
1686	76.8	1723	101.0		
1687	70.9	1724	92.7	1760	91.5
1688	82.9	1725	93.5	1761	84.6
1689	82.9	1726	94.3	1762	90.2

31

Table 2 (Continued)

Year	Index	Year	Index	Year	Index
1763	99.2	1800	163.1	1837	101.9
1764	100.2	1801	168.2	1838	105.7
1765	100.9	1802	132.0	1839	112.7
1766	101.7	1803	133.5		
1767	97.2	1804	134.3	1840	110.7
1768	96.9	1805	147.1	1841	105.5
1769	92.3	1806	145.3	1842	95.9
		1807	141.7	1843	86.1
1770	93.1	1808	156.1	1844	87.6
1771	100.7	1809	167.4	1845	90.0
1772	102.7			1846	92.9
1773	102.2	1810	165.7	1847	104.6
1774	102.1	1811	157.1	1848	88.4
1775	104.2	1812	176.8	1849	79.8
1776	105.3	1813	182.5		
1777	92.2	1814	166.0	1850	79.4
1778	90.7	1815	140.3	1851	77.3
1779	87.2	1816	128.1	1852	80.4
		1817	142.5	1853	97.9
1780	88.3	1818	149.8	1854	105.2
1781	89.7	1819	138.4	1855	104.1
1782	98.1			1856	104.1
1783	95.4	1820	124.7	1857	108.2
1784	90.1	1821	107.7	1858	93.8
1785	89.3	1822	95.0	1859	96.9
1786	90.6	1823	105.4		
1787	95.9	1824	110.1	1860	102.1
1788	90.7	1825	122.1	1861	101.0
1789	96.7	1826	108.0	1862	104.1
		1827	107.3	1863	106.2
1790	96.5	1828	104.1	1864	108.2
1791	96.9	1829	103.5	1865	104.1
1792	95.2			1866	105.2
1793	104.4	1830	102.1	1867	103.1
1794	106.4	1831	102.9	1868	102.1
1795	124.1	1832	98.8	1869	101.0
1796	125.4	1833	95.7		
1797	114.7	1834	93.4	1870	99.0
1798	116.6	1835	91.3	1871	103.1
1799	134.6	1836	102.8	1872	112.4

Table 2 (Continued)

Year	Index	Year	Index	Year	Index
1873	114.4	1908	75.3	1942	
1874	105.2	1909	76.3	1943	
1875	99.0			1944	
1876	97.9	1910	80.4	1945	
1877	96.9	1911	82.5	1946	162.0
1878	89.7	1912	87.6	1947	177.4
1879	85.6	1913	87.6	1948	202.8
		1914	87.6	1949	212.7
1880	90.7	1915	111.3		
1881	87.6	1916	140.2	1950	248.0
1882	86.6	1917	184.5	1951	365.7
1883	84.5	1918	197.9	1952	375.1
1884	78.4	1919	212.4	1953	375.5
1885	74.2			1954	377.8
1886	71.1	1920	258.8	1955	389.4
1887	70.1	1921	159.8	1956	406.1
1888	72.2	1922	135.1	1957	419.0
1889	74.2	1923	133.0	1958	421.7
		1924	143.3	1959	423.2
1890	74.2	1925	140.2		
1891	74.2	1926	129.9	1960	428.9
1892	70.1	1927	125.8	1961	440.3
1893	70.1	1928	123.7	1962	450.1
1894	64.9	1929	118.6	1963	456.2
1895	63.9			1964	471.4
1896	62.9	1930	100.0	1965	493.1
1897	63.9	1931	85.6	1966	506.8
1898	66.0	1932	82.5	1967	513.3
1899	70.1	1933	81.4	1968	536.1
		1934	84.5	1969	557.0
1900	77.3	1935	86.6		
1901	72.2	1936	91.8	1970	596.3
1902	71.1	1937	105.2	1971	650.0
1903	74.1	1938	93.8	1972	684.6
1904	72.2	1939		1973	734.7
1905	74.2			1974	906.4
1906	79.4	1940		1975	1125.3
1907	82.5	1941		1976	1248.4
					. . . .

Table 3

THE INDEX OF PURCHASING POWER OF GOLD

England 1560–1976

(1930 = 100.0)

Year	Index	Year	Index	Year	Index
1560	174.5	1591	120.5	1622	128.1
1561	163.8	1592	116.6	1623	133.7
1562	271.6	1593	114.7	1624	130.8
1563	174.9	1594	111.0	1625	129.8
1564	218.1	1595	136.0	1626	128.6
1565	169.8	1596	126.4	1627	121.6
1566	143.3	1597	127.1	1628	117.6
1567	140.7	1598	129.7	1629	121.5
1568	140.7	1599	124.3		
1569	144.2			1630	119.7
		1600	124.8	1631	117.1
1570	145.1	1601	125.1	1632	117.9
1571	141.9	1602	111.4	1633	118.1
1572	150.1	1603	122.9	1634	114.6
1573	142.4	1604	132.9	1635	114.4
1574	145.1	1605	126.0	1636	114.7
1575	154.8	1606	123.2	1637	111.6
1576	153.4	1607	120.1	1638	115.2
1577	155.1	1608	118.6	1639	115.7
1578	157.9	1609	121.8		
1579	156.9			1640	109.7
		1610	120.4	1641	95.3
1580	152.1	1611	126.2	1642	108.8
1581	152.7	1612	128.7	1643	114.4
1582	152.4	1613	127.3	1644	113.2
1583	139.9	1614	122.9	1645	111.1
1584	144.5	1615	125.1	1646	106.1
1585	143.3	1616	126.6	1647	95.4
1586	122.5	1617	125.8	1648	96.4
1587	122.9	1618	123.6	1649	92.4
1588	121.4	1619	129.2		
1589	121.0			1650	97.6
		1620	129.0	1651	97.8
1590	120.7	1621	128.4	1652	91.9

34

Table 3 (Continued)

Year	Index	Year	Index	Year	Index
1653	97.7	1690	109.1	1727	107.3
1654	98.8	1691	114.4	1728	107.3
1655	96.8	1692	107.0	1729	113.5
1656	93.7	1693	106.8		
1657	92.2	1694	104.0	1730	111.4
1658	88.4	1695	101.1	1731	111.4
1659	99.6	1696	118.3	1732	116.9
		1697	120.6	1733	122.2
1660	105.2	1698	118.0	1734	122.8
1661	101.9	1699	117.1	1735	118.6
1662	105.9			1736	124.2
1663	115.1	1700	123.1	1737	124.5
1664	114.9	1701	119.1	1738	123.9
1665	108.7	1702	125.5	1739	115.7
1666	112.1	1703	123.7		
1667	115.5	1704	118.6	1740	99.4
1668	121.3	1705	117.1	1741	101.1
1669	125.1	1706	118.9	1742	107.6
		1707	117.6	1743	109.6
1670	121.6	1708	114.0	1744	108.4
1671	122.4	1709	110.4	1745	105.5
1672	119.3			1746	95.1
1673	117.2	1710	103.4	1747	105.2
1674	118.5	1711	107.6	1748	104.4
1675	128.1	1712	104.5	1749	115.8
1676	120.2	1713	104.3		
1677	119.1	1714	103.5	1750	112.7
1678	126.8	1715	104.4	1751	113.5
1679	119.0	1716	103.8	1752	119.6
		1717	103.2	1753	116.9
1680	117.5	1718	103.2	1754	113.2
1681	115.9	1719	96.4	1755	111.7
1682	116.2			1756	108.5
1683	114.6	1720	115.7	1757	108.4
1684	110.0	1721	108.4	1758	107.8
1685	113.1	1722	109.5	1759	108.5
1686	123.3	1723	98.5		
1687	133.6	1724	107.3	1760	110.8
1688	114.2	1725	106.4	1761	121.4
1689	114.2	1726	105.5	1762	113.6

Table 3 (Continued)

Year	Index	Year	Index	Year	Index
1763	104.1	1800	66.9	1837	97.9
1764	101.2	1801	65.6	1838	94.4
1765	99.2	1802	80.7	1839	88.6
1766	99.9	1803	76.9		
1767	105.1	1804	76.5	1840	90.2
1768	105.3	1805	69.8	1841	94.6
1769	111.6	1806	70.7	1842	104.1
		1807	72.5	1843	115.9
1770	110.7	1808	65.8	1844	113.9
1771	101.7	1809	69.5	1845	110.9
1772	100.0			1846	107.4
1773	97.8	1810	71.3	1847	95.4
1774	97.5	1811	81.7	1848	112.9
1775	97.6	1812	78.4	1849	125.1
1776	94.6	1813	75.9		
1777	108.0	1814	85.1	1850	125.7
1778	109.8	1815	96.1	1851	129.1
1779	114.1	1816	80.2	1852	124.1
		1817	70.7	1853	101.9
1780	112.7	1818	69.8	1854	94.9
1781	110.9	1819	75.1	1855	95.9
1782	101.7			1856	95.9
1783	103.6	1820	80.2	1857	92.2
1784	111.0	1821	92.9	1858	106.4
1785	112.0	1822	104.6	1859	103.0
1786	109.8	1823	94.3		
1787	103.8	1824	90.3	1860	97.7
1788	109.7	1825	81.7	1861	98.8
1789	102.9	1826	92.0	1862	95.9
		1827	92.6	1863	94.0
1790	103.1	1828	95.5	1864	92.2
1791	102.7	1829	96.4	1865	95.9
1792	104.5			1866	94.9
1793	95.3	1830	97.7	1867	96.8
1794	93.5	1831	97.0	1868	97.7
1795	80.2	1832	101.0	1869	98.8
1796	79.3	1833	104.3		
1797	87.2	1834	106.9	1870	100.8
1798	85.8	1835	109.3	1871	96.8
1799	74.1	1836	97.1	1872	88.8

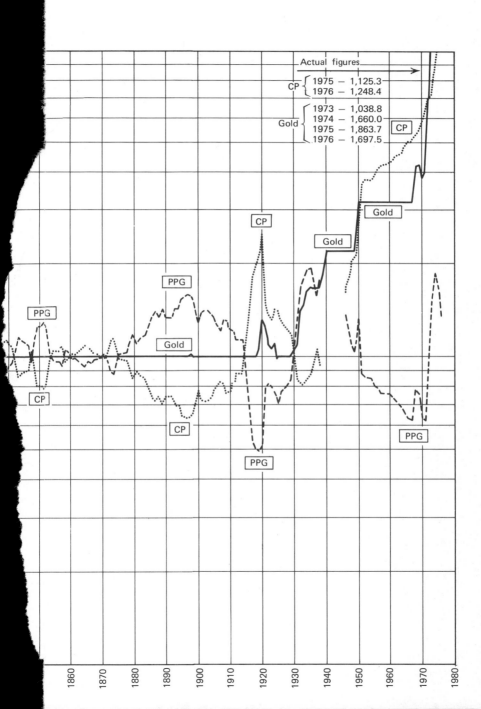

Actual figures

CP { 1975 — 1,125.3
     1976 — 1,248.4

Gold { 1973 — 1,038.8
        1974 — 1,660.0
        1975 — 1,863.7
        1976 — 1,697.5

CP

CP

Gold

Gold

Gold

PPG

PPG

PPG

PPG

CP

CP

PPG

PPG

1860 1870 1880 1890 1900 1910 1920 1930 1940 1950 1960 1970 1980

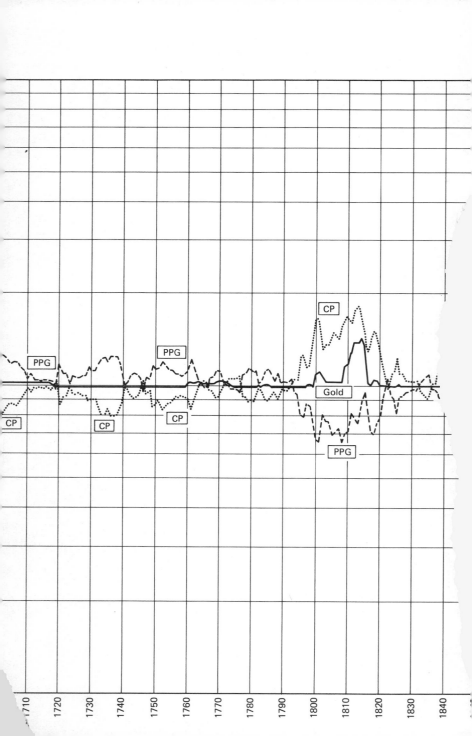

Chart I **The English Experience:** Indexes of the Price of Gold, Commodities, and Purchasing Power, 1560–1976: 1930=100.0

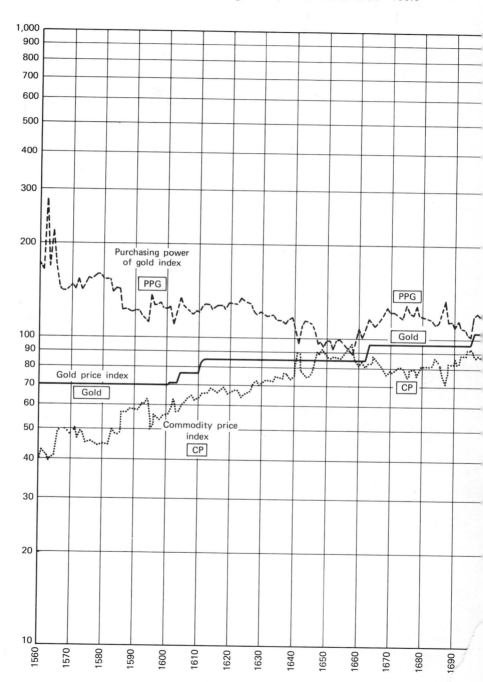

Table 3 (Continued)

Year	Index	Year	Index	Year	Index
1873	87.2	1908	132.7	1942	
1874	94.9	1909	130.8	1943	
1875	100.8			1944	
1876	101.9	1910	124.1	1945	
1877	103.0	1911	121.0	1946	136.2
1878	111.3	1912	113.9	1947	124.4
1879	116.6	1913	113.9	1948	108.8
		1914	113.9	1949	103.8
1880	110.0	1915	89.7		
1881	113.9	1916	71.2	1950	128.7
1882	115.2	1917	54.1	1951	87.3
1883	118.1	1918	50.4	1952	85.1
1884	127.3	1919	49.9	1953	85.0
1885	134.5			1954	84.5
1886	140.4	1920	51.4	1955	81.9
1887	142.4	1921	78.8	1956	78.6
1888	138.2	1922	81.3	1957	76.2
1889	134.5	1923	79.8	1958	75.7
		1924	76.9	1959	75.4
1890	134.5	1925	70.8		
1891	134.6	1926	76.9	1960	74.6
1892	142.5	1927	79.4	1961	72.5
1893	142.5	1928	80.8	1962	70.9
1894	153.8	1929	84.2	1963	69.9
1895	156.2			1964	67.7
1896	158.8	1930	100.0	1965	64.7
1897	156.5	1931	127.1	1966	63.0
1898	151.4	1932	168.4	1967	62.2
1899	142.4	1933	180.5	1968	78.1
		1934	191.6	1969	75.5
1900	129.2	1935	193.1		
1901	138.2	1936	179.8	1970	63.5
1902	140.5	1937	157.4	1971	62.3
1903	140.4	1938	178.7	1972	91.0
1904	138.4	1939		1973	141.4
1905	134.5			1974	183.2
1906	125.8	1940		1975	165.6
1907	121.1	1941		1976	136.0
				...	....

2 Historical Fluctuations in the Price of Gold

1343–1976: THE BROAD SWEEP

Because an ounce of gold, fine or standard, has been so well defined for so long, I feel free to carry its prices back further than for other commodities. This will be done, however, only under the stricture laid down by Beveridge, namely, that the time series come from the same source.*

The figures in Table 4 are adapted from Feaveryear, *The Pound Sterling*, Appendix II, beginning with 1343. The gold prices are in shillings per *fine* ounce, and a column has been added that puts these on an index base of 1930 = 100.0, as for the index numbers in Table 1.

*I feel uneasy about price citations from very early times, for example, 500 B.C. or even 200A.D. These are almost necessarily from different sources, certainly different from recent ones, and usually the degree of purity of metal is not defined. They may be interesting fragments of information, but not trustworthy for statistical analysis.

Table 4

GOLD PRICES IN ENGLAND

1343–1549

Year	Gold Price, Fine in Shillings	Gold Price Index 1930=100.0
1343	24.72	17.4
1344	22.79	16.0
1345	22.91	16.1
1346	23.98	16.9
1351	25.98	18.2
1355	26.28	18.5
1363	26.36	18.6
1412	29.34	20.7
1464	32.78	23.1
1465	38.36	27.0
1467	38.92	27.4
1471	39.54	27.8
1492	39.98	28.2
Aug. 1526	45.00	31.7
May 1544	48.00	33.8
Mar. 1545	50.00	35.2
Jan. 1546	51.00	35.9
Mar. 1546	51.00	35.9
Oct. 1546	52.00	36.6
Jan. 1547	58.00	40.8
1549	60.00	42.3

We now can visualize 633 years of gold price history by considering Tables 1 and 4 together.

In the broadest possible sweep, what we see is a continuous, rather gradual, rise in the index for 360 years until about 1700. Then there are approximately 230 years of essentially stable prices, terminating in 1930, during most of which time England was on the gold standard. Next we see 45 years of utter instability in the price of gold, quite unprecedented in recorded history.

1343–1700: THE LONG CLIMB TO THE GOLD STANDARD

Before 1492, of course, bullion from the Americas had not entered even Spain. The rise in gold prices reflected in England by more than 60 percent from 1343–1492 was due fundamentally to an increase in the demand for gold to support rising levels of commercial activity in Europe in the face of essentially static stocks of the metal. The effects of this competition for gold are graphically described by Feavearyear in his second chapter, "The Struggle for Bullion."

European commerce was severely impeded by the sparse supply of gold and silver. Economic development had come almost to a standstill and the prospect for expansion was dim. It is sobering to speculate on what the world might—or more properly, might not—have become if the treasures of the Americas had not been discovered when they were.

In 1519 Cortez marched on Mexico City. In 1534 Pizarro returned to Spain with the first treasure from Peru. Early supplies of gold objects and ornaments from the Aztecs and Incas were soon supplemented by bullions from the mines.

In 1545 the rich deposits at Potosi in Peru began to supply silver, and in 1555 these were joined by the discoveries at Guanajuato in Mexico. During the sixteenth century 181,235 kilograms (199.4 tons) of gold and 16,632,648 kilograms (18,246 tons) of silver reached Spain as a matter of official record. We have no idea how much else was delivered to Europe by smugglers or by pirates.

The effects spread quickly throughout Europe as a result of the pride of Carlos V of Spain. With the treasure from the New World in very good supply, the government of Spain showed commendable concern for the quality of its coinage. The reals, escudos, and coronas were of consistently high bullion content, and merchants all over Europe were eager to trade for them. In this way the bullion of the Americas spread its effects quickly throughout the Continent and into Britain.

Signature: _____

Black			
Blue			
White			
Red			
Handicap	1	3	

As early as 1523 the Cortes of Valladolid urged Charles V to reduce the gold and silver content, "so that by these means they will no longer draw our gold from the kingdom." It was 14 years before Charles acted, and inflationary pressures were exported meanwhile, along with the good bullion content. Even then he remarked with pride that he had lost his Spanish coins only because they were so good.

In spite of the dramatic romanticism of the Spanish Main and treasure ships, the supply of new gold from the New World was just a trickle by later standards. Less than 1 percent of what was to be 1930 world production was produced in each of the years from 1500 to 1520. The price of gold continued to rise (but at a diminished rate) as demand continued to outstrip supply.

If we look at "World Production of Gold" in Appendix C we see that the annual volume for 1521–1544 was 1.1 percent of the 1930 base period, that 1545–1560 saw this stepped up to 1.3 percent, but that new production settled back to 1.1 percent for the next 40 years.

From 1600 to 1700 there was a persistent rise in the world production index to 1.7 percent. In spite of the rise in supply, the price of gold climbed to a level in 1700 below which it has never fallen since. The tremendous surges of new supplies from California, Australia, Alaska, Russia, and South Africa were never to break that price again. It would go as low, but never appreciably lower, in the next 275 years.

1700-1800: THE GOLD STANDARD AND STABILITY

England slid onto the gold standard in 1717 in the manner described in Chapter 1. Thereafter, prices remained constant at 77.5 shillings until 1760, by the best evidence we have from the Bank of England's buying price.

In 1760 gold prices broke upward in the market and remained higher than the Bank buying price until 1773. This episode can be attributed to two phenomena: (a) the sorry state of gold coinage in the mid-eighteenth century and its rehabilitation by the Recoinage of 1774, and (b) the rapid development of country banks after 1750 and the emergence of the Bank of England as a bank of final reserve.

Let us look at these in turn. In an attempt to rehabilitate the debased coinage of earlier years, the Act of 1698 had provided that anyone receiving deficient silver coins should deface them with a provision for removing them from circulation. The remedy was for the prevalent silver coins of those days and was not made to apply to the rarer gold.

After the coinage of gold had risen to very substantial volume following the gold standard of 1717, gold coins in circulation became progressively lighter. As a result, all full-weight ones were exported as soon as minted, and the market price of gold began to climb.

By 1773 nearly all the gold coinage was circulating on a debased basis, and the Act of 1698 was extended from silver to include gold coins as well. This time the Act had teeth in it: severe penalties were provided for passing on debased coins. By arrangement, the Bank of England purchased defaced coins by weight at the Mint price. This effectively brought the market price of gold down to official levels by 1774.

The debasement-rehabilitation model just described was enough to account for gold's price behavior between 1760 and 1774. But a parallel phenomenon accentuated the rise of gold prices after the 1750s. This was the rapid growth of the so-called country banks. These were institutions outside London and in places like Sussex, Essex, Norfolk, Suffolk, and Hull. Only about a dozen of these existed in 1750, but by 1793 there were almost 400.

At this early date the framework of a modern banking system was established, with rapidly expanding credit issues. The importance for our present study is that the stock of golden guineas in the Bank of England was the final reserve for all these credit issues and had to be expanded rapidly. This generated a new surge in the demand for gold with an attendant rise in price. (These events are fully described in Sir John Clapham's *The Bank of England*.)

The pronounced growth of industry, trade, commerce, and banking in the second half of the eighteenth century brought with it the business cycle in the modern sense. We have not been freed of business cycles since.

There were the crises of 1763, 1772, 1775, 1783, and the panic of 1793. The latter was ignited and fed by the sudden declaration of war on England by France in February. In the financial chaos that followed, the credit of the burgeoning system of country banks utterly collapsed. The pressure on the Bank of England in the role of final reserve was tremendous. Her stock of bullion swiftly fell by 50 percent. Even so, gold weathered all these crises without drastic price reactions. The system was invincibly resilient. Gold prices held firm until 1800 when stability was shattered. It was not until 1820 that they were to settle back to a steady state.

1800-1820: NAPOLEON AND THE AFTERMATH

When gold coins circulate freely and paper money can be exchanged for gold at face value, the market price of gold can never get far from the Mint price. These conditions maintained from 1774 until 1798. And with the Mint price constant, the market price held fairly level.

Then the requisite conditions just stated began to fall apart.

First, recall that England was at war with France. An early symptom of the times to come was when common people began to withdraw guineas from their banks and bury them in pastures and gardens (see *The Times* for December 1796 and January 1797). The internal gold drain had begun. The run on the banks became so great that on Sunday, February 26, 1797, an Order in Council was issued stating:

It is indispensably necessary for the public service that the Directors of the Bank of England should forbear issuing any cash in payment until the sense of the Parliament can be taken on that subject and the proper measures adopted thereupon for maintaining the means of circulation.

For all practical purposes England was off the gold standard. No constraint remained on the supply of paper money except the wisdom and resolve of the Directors of the Bank of England. Both of these were weak.

No one in the Bank or government seemed to consider himself at all responsible for regulating the supply of money, let alone paper currency. Even worse, no one showed any sign of appreciating the *need* for such regulation.

As the Directors later publicly stated, the Bank of England did not force its notes on the public. It merely supplied the public demand. How, therefore, could the Directors be accused of issuing too much paper?

Other banks claimed equal innocence. The overriding position was that although there was no forcing of paper money on the public, there was little limitation on those who asked for it. Unrestricted credit was made available with paper. Whenever public demand went up, either for legitimate business purposes or sheer speculation, the Bank satisfied it with further paper issue.

The first shock of the unregulated pound hit the commodity markets in 1799. As we see in Table 2, our index of commodity prices jumped from 116.6 in 1798 to 134.6 in 1799, then soared to 163.1 in 1800, to top off at 168.2 in the following year (1930 = 100.0). The first great inflation in 150 years was under way.

The overheated economy finally fell back a little, and some degree of price stability at this higher level was attained until the boom of 1808–1813. The new attack on the value of the pound struck from sources that have never been clearly identified. The beginning of the Peninsular War certainly stimulated optimism in England and an increased demand for military supplies. Current press accounts suggested that Napoleon's time was running out. But also in 1808 the Portuguese monopoly of trade with Brazil was broken, and English commerce quickly moved in there.

The spirit of private venture prevailed. Anyone who wanted to get in on the action with some borrowed capital could bring his paper to the Bank of England for discounting and the Directors could see no reason for refusing. It was public demand, so what could be the harm? The proliferating country banks followed the example. Our commodity price index shows that prices went from 141.7 in 1807 to 167.4 in 1809, and topped off at 182.5 in 1813. Prices on the Continent were soaring, too.

All this had a predictable effect on the market price of gold in London. Its index went from 100.0 in 1798 to 109.1 in 1800 and climbed thereafter to a peak of 141.2 in 1814.

It may seem that with this rise in the price of gold, ownership of the metal was a sure haven against the inflation of the paper currency of the times, that operational wealth would be preserved. But this was not the case, as we see in Chapter 5.

It would be facile to attribute the commodity price inflation and the soaring price of bullion simply to the Napoleonic Wars. As we have seen, this period was also marked by monetary mismanagement and aggravated by hyperactive commercial venturism.

The effect on gold markets was further heightened by what was happening in France. There the paper currency—the assignat—crashed to zero for all practical purposes in early 1795. The French Government resolved to go on the gold standard. As usual, the French people reacted to gold with fervor. There was a swift revival of confidence among the people, and they began transferring their savings home. The good gold, which had been driven out of circulation by the bad assignat, rushed back. The metal was drained away from the rest of the world, and especially England, with a consequent effect on bullion prices there.

What was allowed to happen to the currency during the

period just discussed came as a profound shock to the monetary establishment of the day. This was not the ancient deviltry of debasement. A more subtle evil was afoot—inflation of a paper currency.

In August 1809 David Ricardo wrote the first of his famous three letters to the *Morning Chronicle*. He argued that it was the overissue of bank notes that was putting a premium on gold in the market. Soon after, a committee of the Commons was appointed to inquire into the high price of gold bullion. This came, not surprisingly, to be known as the "Bullion Committee."

The central conclusion that the Bullion Committee drew from long study of all the facts was that the rise in the price of bullion had been caused solely by overissues of Bank of England notes.

The intriguing feature is that the committee did not really blame the Directors of the Bank of England for what had occurred. In testimony before the Committee both the Governor and the Deputy Governor had expressed very strongly the view that the Bank's notes could not have been overissued, since they were issued only in response to public demand. Obviously then, they could not be faulted.

The Bullion Committee, although making an adverse judgment, simply regarded the Directors as men who had had a greater responsibility thrust on them than anyone could be expected to bear. In what amounted to exoneration by reason of incompetence, the Bullion Committee report stated:

> The suspension of cash payments has had the effect of committing into the hands of the Directors of the Bank of England, to be exercised by their sole discretion, the immediate charge of supplying the country with that quantity of circulating medium which is exactly proportioned to the wants and occasions of the Public. In the judgment of the Committee that is a trust which it is unreasonable to expect that the Directors of the Bank of England should ever be able to discharge. The most detailed knowledge of the actual trade of the Country, combined with the profound Science in all principles of Money and circulation, would not allow any man

or set of men to adjust, and keep always adjusted, the right proportion of circulating medium in a country to the wants of trade.

Because in the United States today the Federal Reserve Board has ultimate governance of the supply of money, its Open Market Committee can take some solace from the Bullion Committee's report.

By the end of 1813 the paper money in circulation was at its highest level, commodity prices had reached their peak at 57 percent above the index level of 116.6 which had prevailed in 1798, and gold was as high as it was ever to touch again until 1932 (138.6).

As the power of Napoleon began to decline, the prices of commodities and gold began to recede. In the year of peace before the return of Napoleon from exile, finance and commerce tottered along, the reopening of continental markets probably forestalling the effects of the collapse of war industries. When the war broke out again the old conditions returned for the Hundred Days. Waterloo put a final end to Napoleon's hope, and in 1815 the British economy began a decline.

The next notable event in the gold story was the passage of Liverpool's Act of 1816. This stated for the first time in statutory form that gold coin should henceforth be the sole standard measure of value and that the existing standard weight and fineness of the gold coins should remain. Further, if gold coins of any other denominations than those already in use came to be, they should be of proportionate weight.

A new coin was circulated in July 1817. It was the sovereign at 20 shillings, weighing "five pennyweights, three grains 2740/10,000 troy weight of standard gold," or 20/21 of the weight of a guinea.

Just a century after the establishment of the guinea at 21 shillings in effect ushered in the gold standard, that venerable coin was replaced by the gold sovereign. The great economic expansion of the eighteenth century had rested on the guinea, and the sovereign was to serve the nineteenth century in a similar way.

The Liverpool Act seemed to foreshadow the resumption of specie payment. But an odd sort of vacillation set in for the next few years. A reading of the record gives the impression that everyone was in favor of the end of inconvertible paper—some day, but not just yet.

Finally in 1819 the House appointed the "Committee on Expediency of the Bank Resuming Cash Payments." Sir Robert Peel was named Chairman.

It was finally Peel's speech to the House that carried the day. Curiously, Peel had voted against the Bullion Committee in 1811. But now, like a reformed sinner, he went all the way to expound "sound" money. He proposed a return to "the ancient standard" as soon as possible. To him the pound was a definite piece of metal, effectively fixed by the proclamation of 1717. Common honesty, he said, dictated that England should return to that standard. John Locke lived again!

Peel rallied the brains of the House of Lords behind him and carried England back to the gold standard at 3 pounds, 17 shillings, 10.5 pence with very little opposition. Peel's Act placed England on a gold standard more nearly automatic in its workings than the world had seen before or since. No Mint charges existed, and minting was free and open to all. The introduction of the milled coin in 1663 had defeated the clipper. Improved technology in the Mint and better enforcement of the relevant laws began to defeat the counterfeiter. The act abolished restrictions on melting and exporting gold coin. There were no limits on gold to go in or out of the country. The Bank, acting for the Mint, was prepared to buy all the bullion brought to it. With the slightest fall in the price of gold elsewhere large quantities flowed to England. With the smallest fall of the purchasing power of currency in England large quantities of gold poured out.

The price of gold remained very nearly constant for a century. The classical gold standard was at work.

1914-1946: TWO WARS AND THE GREAT DEPRESSION

World War I was the first war to mobilize whole nations. Even the Napoleonic Wars placed limited demands on national resources, and civilian populations conducted much of their economic lives by normal methods.

But in England the First World War called on all her resources either for use in active fighting or for the war industries. Civil consumption was cut to the minimum.

The first economic shock had somewhat worn off by the end of 1914. Legally, paper was still convertible into gold, and gold could still be exported. What actually went out of the country was the minimum necessary for settling international balances and was exported mainly in warships. The London price of gold did not rise all through the war.

When artificial support for the sterling-dollar exchange rate was removed in March 1919, sterling fell sharply in relation to the dollar. With war risks to bullion shipment no longer present, the fall of sterling would have normally induced large outflows of gold. Confronted with this possibility, those in charge decided to maintain the appearance of a gold standard, even if they removed its substance. Paper money remained legally convertible, but the export of gold by private parties was forbidden.

From 1919 until the conversion to a new form of gold standard in April 1925, London was the gold market through which passed the bullion of the Empire (mainly South African) to the rest of the world. Since most of this was to America (the creditor nation), the dominant influence on the London gold price was the sterling-dollar exchange rate. Thus gold rapidly rose to a premium over the Mint price.

Foreshadowed by a speech by Chancellor Winston Churchill on April 28, England went on to what is now known as the "gold-bullion" standard with the Gold Standard Act of 1925. Its main provisions should be carefully noted:

1. It repealed all sections of all previous statutes that made paper money payable in gold coin.
2. It denied the right of free access to the Mint.
3. It obligated the Bank of England to sell gold only in bars with a minimum weight of approximately 400 troy ounces at the historic price of 3 pounds, 17 shillings, 10.5 pence.

An institution that has lived for 200 years does not die easily. Even as a cripple, the standard of gold had seemed worth keeping alive. One authority has referred to it as "the international gold standard façade" (W. Adams Brown, Jr., *The International Gold Standard Reinterpreted*, p. 391).

What the Act of 1925 did do, however, was to bring the London market price of gold down to the old level and keep it there until 1931.

Thus Winston Churchill paid his allegiance to John Locke and the time-honored 3 pounds, 17 shillings, 10.5 pence. As Keynes put it later, "It was an automatic and painful act."

When Great Britain returned to this new version of the gold standard, she was accompanied by The Netherlands, Hungary, Australia, New Zealand, and South Africa. Others moved on shortly thereafter, and before the end of 1928, this new form of the gold standard was in place in nearly all the countries that had had a gold standard before the war.

But whatever the intent of governments, the smooth working of the gold standard of the nineteenth century was not to be again. One change was in the global distribution of monetary gold—in 1913 European countries held 54 percent, North America 24 percent, and Britain 9 percent. By 1925 North America had risen to 45 percent, continental Europe had fallen to 28 percent, and Britain was getting along with 7 percent (now wholly concentrated in the Bank of England). This situation was to become further aggravated by a heavy flow into the United States after 1928.

Then, before all the financial problems that were a legacy of World War I could be sorted out, let alone solved, the Great

Depression hit. On Saturday, September 19, 1931, the British government decided to suspend the gold standard completely. Parliament pushed through the enabling act on Monday the twenty-first.

As mentioned before, old institutions die hard. The Parliamentary bill was named the Gold Standard (Amendment) Act of 1931, but it amended Britain's gold standard right out of existence. The crucial clause read, "Until His Majesty by Proclamation otherwise directs subsection 2 of section one of the Gold Standard Act, 1925 shall cease to have effect." This was the key subsection requiring the Bank to sell gold.

The 8 years between the suspension of the gold standard and the outbreak of World War II in Europe were years of great confusion on the foreign exchange markets. The unbalanced distribution of the world's gold became even more marked; large movements of monetary stocks from one center to another occurred because of political tensions and motivations rather than purely economic reasons. Nations competed with each other in devaluing their currencies. The market price of gold rocketed by 82 percent between 1930 and 1939 (see Chart I).

One strong impetus to change was a drastic shift in the policy of the United States in 1933. In March the United States imposed an embargo on gold exports and effectively went off the gold standard (see Chapter 6).

Then, in the second half of 1933, the United States government began buying gold at ever-increasing prices. Starting with $20.67 per ounce, the price climbed to $35.00 in early 1934, at which point it was stabilized. This increase was for the purely internal purpose of raising domestic commodity prices (at which it failed), but it had serious impact on the gold markets of the world.

Turbulent times for gold set in and continued through the Second World War. But neither these nor the centuries preceding prepared gold markets for what was to come.

A history of gold during this period requires reference to the Bretton Woods Conference and the founding of the International Monetary Fund. The Conference was convened in July 1944, and the agreement that established the International Monetary Fund became effective in December 1946. A nation's membership in the Fund was based on its "quota"—something like shares in a corporation, and a denominator for its voting rights.

A basic question that faced the new organization was the choice of monetary unit which would serve as the common denominator for the quotas. The Fund Agreement chose the dollar of the United States as defined on July 1, 1945, namely 15 5/21 grains of gold, 9/10 fine. Thus the dollar—defined in gold, notice—became the central monetary unit of the non-Soviet world. (There is extensive, specialized literature on the International Monetary Fund. A good place to start is with an excellent book by Arthur Nussbaum, *A History of the Dollar*, Columbia University Press, New York, 1957.)

1948-1976: A PERIOD THAT CANNOT YET BE LABELED

In 1948 the first free market for gold reopened in Paris, followed in 1952 by the removal by the Swiss of the price ceiling on gold traded in that country. The free market in London reopened in 1954.

In November 1961 eight of the most powerful central banks had entered into a consortium known as the London Gold Pool. The aim of this agreement was to stabilize the free market at $35.0875, the gold export point at New York City. The modus operandi was to buy when the price fell and sell when it rose (the countries were the United States, Britain, France, West Germany, Italy, Switzerland, Belgium, and The Netherlands). For the next 4 years they succeeded in maintaining the price at the target level.

In the early part of 1965, the demand for gold in the London market was stronger than at any time since its reopening in

1954. In March, for example, the market price was $35.17. Then the successful consortium began to break up.

In 1966 the Soviet Union ceased selling gold on the world market. Total production of the free world remained almost constant from the year before at 41.2 million ounces. Private demand for gold was still increasing, and, for the first time, the eight central banks in the London Gold Pool were forced to sell from their national reserves to keep the price down to the target level.

Speculative fever began to run high. As one indication, the price of gold coins in Paris increased by 11.4 percent from the end of May to the close of December 1966. Then on January 31, 1967, with demand exceedingly intense, France abruptly removed the ban on the private import of gold by its citizens. This gave a tremendous boost to the effective demand for bullion. In June the Bank of France capped it all by precipitously withdrawing from the London Gold Pool itself.

On March 17, 1968 the London Gold Pool was dissolved, and the "two-tier" gold market emerged. Thereafter, monetary gold would be used for official settlements only within a closed system of central banks. The United States agreed to sell to other nations from its own gold reserve only when necessary to settle their obligations to the International Monetary Fund. This was the first tier, with the price maintained at $35.00 by the United States. The other tier was for private buyers who could purchase freely on open markets at prices set by supply and demand. The demand was tremendous, and the price results can be read from Chart I.

Chart I is instructive because the postgold standard gyration following 1931 can be judged vividly against the background of stability that had existed for more than 200 years.

In a single year gold prices leaped by an astounding amount equalling the full rise of the Napoleonic Wars. And that was only the start. Looking at the full sweep of four centuries in Chart I, one can appreciate the unique character of the last 7 years. The surge in price is unparalleled in recorded history. But for a better appreciation of the forces at work, let us turn to the detail of Chart II, which focuses on the return to free markets in 1948 and thereafter.

Perhaps the most authoritative, privately issued analysis of the gold markets is the annual publication of Consolidated Gold Field Limited, written and edited by Peter D. Fells. The following table is reproduced from *Gold 1976* and forms the basis for Chart II.

On Chart II the broken line represents net private purchases of bullion and the solid line uppermost shows total purchases [i.e., the sum in each year of Official Purchases (or Sales) and Net Private Purchases in Table 5]. There is no need to plot Total Supplies, because gold is one commodity for which total purchases (including central banks) equal total supplies. The line with dots represents the London market price of gold on the index number basis of Table 1.

The effect of the events leading up to the dissolution of the London Gold Pool and the subsequent behavior of the price of gold can now be traced. From the reopening of the London gold market in 1954 through 1961, the price of gold held steady without any overtly orchestrated efforts by the major central banks. Toward the close of the latter year the London Gold Pool was formed for the express purpose of maintaining the price at the United States gold export point of $35.0875. In 1966, for the first time, the members of the Pool had to sell from their reserves to keep the price down. This was in part required to offset the disappearance of Russian gold sales, which had been an ameliorating influence up until then. Sales by pool members are reflected in Chart II by the dip in the total curve *below* the broken line representing private purchases in 1966 and thereafter.

In January 1967 France removed its embargo on gold imports by private citizens. Private purchases (on all accounts) far more than doubled in a single year. In June France aggravated the supply-demand imbalance by withdrawing from the London Gold Pool altogether. By the end of 1967 the seven central banks

Table 5

GOLD BULLION: SUPPLY AND DEMAND

1948–1975

(metric tons)

	Free World Mine Production	Net Trade with Soviet Bloc	Official Purchases (or Sales)	Net Private Purchases	Total
1948	702	—	369	333	702
1949	733	—	369	337	706
1950	755	—	288	467	755
1951	733	—	235	498	733
1952	755	—	205	550	755
1953	755	67	404	418	822
1954	795	67	595	267	862
1955	835	67	591	311	902
1956	871	133	435	569	1004
1957	906	231	614	523	1137
1958	933	196	605	524	1129
1959	1000	266	671	595	1266
1960	1049	177	262	964	1226
1961	1080	266	538	808	1346
1962	1155	178	329	1004	1333
1963	1204	489	729	964	1693
1964	1249	400	631	1018	1649
1965	1280	355	196	1439	1635
1966	1285	−67	−40	1258	1218
1967	1250	−5	−1404	2649	1245
1968	1245	−29	−620	1836	1216
1969	1252	−15	90	1147	1237
1970	1273	−3.2	236	1034	1270
1971	1236	54	−96	1386	1290
1972	1169	213	151	1231	1382
1973	1119	275	−6	1400	1394
1974	1014	220	−20	1254	1234
1975	951	149	−25	1125	1100

Source. Adapted from Peter Fells and Christopher Glynn, *Gold 1976,* Consolidated Gold Fields, Ltd., 1976.

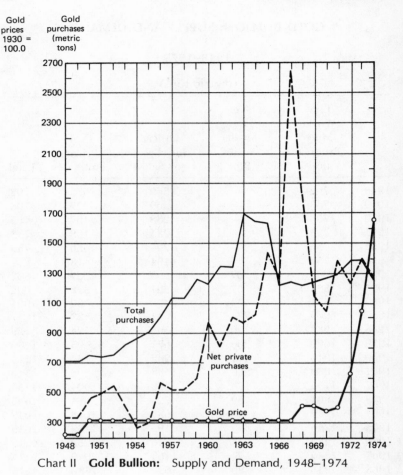

| Gold prices 1930 = 100.0 | Gold purchases (metric tons) |

Chart II   **Gold Bullion:**   Supply and Demand, 1948–1974

remaining in the pool had to sell $1.6 billion in bullion just to keep the London market price at $35.20.

Two and one-half months into 1968, the remaining central banks gave up this collective effort and the price of gold took off on an explosive course unprecedented in monetary history.*

*For an absorbing insider's account of the creation and collapse of the Gold Pool see Charles A. Coombs, the arena of international finance, John Wiley & Sons, 1976, Chapters 4 and 9.

3 Commodity Prices and the Construction of Index Numbers

The first and second chapters have been devoted to the use of gold as money and fluctuations in its price throughout the centuries. But the price of gold alone tells us nothing about what it will *buy*. So we are brought by necessity to the second part of our conceptual equation GP ÷ CP = PPG (the price of gold divided by the price of commodities equals the purchasing power of gold). And PPG deserves a close look, since, as we see, every sharp gyration of the purchasing power of gold coincides with sweeping institutional changes in monetary systems.

How can we construct with confidence a unified series of commodity prices since 1560 to match our gold price series in order to calculate changes in operational wealth? In short, how do we realize our conceptual scheme as described in the Introduction?

We are indeed fortunate to have as a principal source the work published by Lord Beveridge and his associates, *Prices and Wages in England from the Twelfth to the Nineteenth Centuries,* Vol. 1, 1939. A prodigious effort went into this compilation, and a reader of the original is bound to be impressed with the meticulous care used to secure validity. But to my knowledge the Beveridge collection has never been fully utilized.*

Until Beveridge's work the precedent—really the only—collection of English price statistics was that by Thorold Rogers, published in seven volumes between 1866 and 1902. The effective range of this price history is 1259–1702. It falls short of the nineteenth century, a time terminal necessary to link up with modern index numbers of prices.

The Rogers volumes served a generation of economic historians, but it always suffered a severe flaw: he combined isolated records of transactions in many different places as well as at different times. By drawing each year from different places to construct a price series over time, he built in a risk of noncomparability which the user has no way of evaluating.

The great structural virtue that Beveridge cherished was long price series drawn from a single source. For that single source he trusted only the same set of documents compiled for the same purpose over time. By these two criteria he excluded most of the material compiled by Rogers and forewent personal accounts and commercial documents altogether.

Insistence on time series from a common source (and the rejection of isolated entries) aids the price historian in two ways. Obviously it facilitates interpretation. More subtly, it gets the force of human inertia working for him. Once a person, or an institution managed by persons, sets up a system for procuring a specified quality of a good in a customary quantity and on

---

*In the course of this study I have stored the entire Beveridge collection from 1560–1830 on computer. In addition to its utilization for this book, I plan numerous studies in price history on selected topics for publication in journal articles and other media. All annual prices are from Michaelmas (Sept. 29) to Michaelmas (roughly the harvest year).

agreed terms, this procurement system tends to be perpetuated over considerable periods. This sets up a presumption of comparability. It is no guarantee, but it helps. Also, when there is a change it is more likely to be noted down, because it is a change in the system itself and not just a random choice.

The Beveridge collection contains price series for nearly 170 commodities. There is one passage written by Lord Beveridge that is appropriate to quote now because of the subject matter of the present book—the purchasing power of gold:

> Those who are told that a history of prices is in preparation often ask as their first question whether the prices allow for changes in the value of money.
>
> In so far as by this is meant changes in the value of money in relation to commodities; the answer is that the course of prices, as recorded in contemporary money, is itself the record and measure of such changes.
>
> In so far as by change in the value of money is meant change in the silver or gold content of the currency, the answer is that the present work, in addition to prices in contemporary money, gives the means of converting all such prices into bullion equivalents. . . .

It is this last task, which Beveridge left undone, that I wish to carry out in my own way, although my interest in doing so antedates the Beveridge volume of 1939.

The price series all came from viable institutions of a substantial, even venerable, character.

Winchester College
Eton College
Westminster (School and Abbey)
Charterhouse
Sandwich (St. Bartholomew's Hospital)
Greenwich Hospital
Chelsea Hospital
Lord Stewards' Department
Lord Chamberlain's Department

Office of Works
Navy Victualling
Naval Stores

Since Beveridge used only price series for commodities that were purchased over substantial periods by these institutions (most for 50 years or more), we can be sure that his collection is not affected by caprice. The commodities were in the mainstream of commerce on the whole and of a type that was in substantial demand year after year for human consumption or application.

It helps also to remember that we are not seeking a sample of prices representative of all commodity money prices at any cross section in time. Our desideratum instead is to represent fairly *changes* in the prices of goods over time, that is, variations in the general price level. This implies that we seek inclusion of prices that are reflective of broad movements which were taking place. The criterion of reflectivity does not, in itself, require that they be for "important" commodities either in volume of trade or any other economic measure.

It is possible to imagine (although I make no nomination here) a commodity that is trivial by any of the usual economic criteria and yet reflects perfectly by its price fluctuations changes in the price level broadly viewed. At an extreme we could be perfectly well satisfied with a nonprice surrogate variable if only we could trust its price-reflective behavior.

Common sense tells us, however, that we should want large-volume items, not because large volume is a sine qua non of reflective value, but because commodities dealt with in large volume are likely to be buffeted by the winds of trade in the same way as commodities generally would be. To put the negative case, we should probably not want to include rare goods, because they are prone to vagaries of their own in price behavior.

Therefore, there are advantages when dealing with all the uncertainties of price history to be certain at least of the institutions that are the sources of our price materials. Still we must resist the temptation to include price series simply because they are available. The dictum, "Something is better than nothing," can be particularly misguiding here. This temptation, and the will to resist it, varies the further our price research goes back in time. When empirical evidence on prices becomes very scarce, our well-intended desire to utilize what does remain may blind us to its faults and nonreflective character.

The prescription for sample selection really comes down to this: Use common sense and your sensitivity as an economist and statistician. Avoid aberrant sectors of the market and stick to the mainstream of commerce. Do not be inveigled by mere availability. Tell your reader exactly what you have done.

Strangely enough, one of the trickiest problems in the context of this study is what do we want our price index to represent? What is the conceptually correct package of commodities to lay against an ounce of gold when measuring the purchasing power of the latter?

I know of no previous model to guide me. Certainly, I do not want a cost-of-living index. It is hardly relevant to think of a wage earner with an ounce of gold in hand shopping for the "typical" market basket at retail of the goods and services that his family consumes. In fact, retail prices themselves do not seem to represent the level of trade meaningful for the purchasing power of a precious metal.

Wholesale prices are the choice. This jibes well enough with the Beveridge collection in which prices paid by institutions are more nearly like the wholesale prices of today than their modern retail counterparts. Beginning with 1790 my own index constructed from the Beveridge data is appropriately spliced into wholesale price indexes published by others. These are discussed presently. Suffice it to say here that I am seeking for the seventeenth and eighteenth centuries a conceptual counterpart of the wholesale price index published regularly by Her Majesty's Central Statistical Office for contemporary Britain—a general index number of wholesale price movements.

The International Scientific Committee on Price History has established the following strata as sound for studies of historical prices as a group:

I.	Grain and other crops	IX.	Miscellaneous foods
II.	Grain products	X.	Drinks
III.	Livestock, meat, and poultry	XI.	Light, fuel, and so on
IV.	Dairy products, fats, and so on	XII.	Textiles
V.	Fish	XIII.	Hides, skins, and so on
VI.	Vegetables	XIV.	Building materials
VII.	Fruit	XV.	Metals
VIII.	Sugar, spices, and so on	XVI.	Chemicals and miscellaneous

These strata are formulated to assure breadth of coverage. An examination of the Beveridge data recorded in my computer memory shows that as early as 1600 commodities are found in Strata I, III, IX, XI, XII, XIII, XIV, XV, and XVI. By 1660 there is representation in all strata except VI, vegetables, for which the first appearance is in 1671.

The sample actually used in this study is, of course, selected within the Beveridge collection. It is a judgmental sample, because probability sampling would be wholly inappropriate. The principal judgment was in deciding what *not* to use. Without reconstructing all the reasoning, consider two examples: prices from the Lord Chamberlain's Department were excluded in toto. A close reading of Beveridge showed that these were centered almost exclusively on the Monarch's immediate household and hardly could be representative of wholesale prices in general. I must say, the temptation was considerable. I was throwing out data that stretched all the way from 1556 to 1829.

Another example was spices. I judged that these were too rare in those early centuries to be at all representative for my purpose. Other examples of exclusion could be given as well.

Full disclosure is part of the creed of the statistician, but publishers have their space limitations. With deference to the latter the composition of the final sample is detailed for only the one year 1700. The commodities are purposely listed in alphabetical order so that readers readily can ascertain if their candidates are included. Also, the reader can define subgroups (e.g., building materials) of particular interest to him and readily determine their proportionate representation in the sample. The digits following some of the commodities indicate the number of separate price series; otherwise only one price series is included for each commodity named.

The sample starts with a modest dozen of commodities in 1560, but expands to 24 price series as early as 1568.* As newly appearing commodities become available for the sample they are spliced in according to recognized statistical procedures.

THE CONSTRUCTION OF INDEX NUMBERS

The material that follows is intended principally for those specialists who are interested in the methodology of measuring commodity price movements. This includes those scholars who cannot accept the findings of the chapters on the purchasing power of gold until they know how the commodity-value component of that purchasing power was statistically determined.

The general reader can find three points to interest him:

1. Why the particular type of index number used was chosen.

2. Why, with this type of index, weights make little difference in practice and an *un*weighted form is satisfactory for historical use.

3. Why care must be taken in comparing index numbers over long periods of time.

*These are bricks (2), candles (2), charcoal, cheese, cloth, lead, lime (2), pewter, pitch, rabbits, solder, straw, tallow, tar, thrums, tile pins, tiles (plain) (3), tiles (ridge), train oil.

Commodity Series
1700

Ale	Diaper (cloth)	Oatmeal 4
Bacon	Ducks	Oats 2
Bark	Eggs	Peas 2
Barley 3	Faggots	Pitch 2
Bavins 2	Flounder	Pork 3
Beans	Flour 2	Pullets
Beef 7	Geese	Rice 2
Beer 1	Glue	Salmon
Billets 2	Gravel	Salt 3
Bisquits 3	Hair	Sand
Bread 3	Hay	Solder
Bricks 4	Hemp	Straw
Broadcloth	Hops	Sugar 4
Butter 4	Lamb	Tallow
Candles 6	Lard	Tar 2
Canvas	Laths 2	Thrums
Cement	Lead 4	Tile pins
Charcoal 2	Leatherbacks	Tiles (plain) 4
Cheese 4	Lime 4	Tiles (ridge)
Chickens	Linen	Train oil
Cloth 2	Malt 4	Turkey hens
Coal 5	Milk	Veal
Cod	Mutton 5	Whiting
Cream	Nails	Whole deals

The Choice of the Geometric Type of Index Number

There are two general types of index numbers: (a) the average of ratios, and (b) the ratio of aggregates. The average of ratios applied to prices can be represented symbolically simply by

$$\frac{\Sigma(P_1/P_0)}{N}$$

in which for a whole set of commodities P_0 represents separately the price of each commodity in a selected base period and P_1 represents the respective price of each of the same commodities in the "given" period being compared with the base. P_1/P_0 is called the price-ratio or price-relative. In the formula as written we are simply taking the ordinary arithmetic mean (average) of the price relatives. This leads to the perfectly intelligible statement in layman's terms that, for example, "On the average, prices in 1976 were 110% of what they were in 1972," 1976 being the "given" period and 1972 the base period in the application of the formula.

The ratio-of-aggregates type of index applied to the same prices between 1976 and 1972, say, would look like this,

$$\frac{\Sigma P_1}{\Sigma P_0}$$

in which the numerator is simply the sum of the individual prices of the various commodities in 1976, and the denominator is the comparable sum of their prices totalled for 1972. Prices for all commodities are treated in their customary unit of price quotation, per pound, per dozen, per pint, and so on.

Of these two basic types I have chosen to use the average-of-ratios mode, justifications for which I advance shortly. Further attention, therefore, is confined to this type.

In the formula as written for this type I have arbitrarily pictured the familiar arithmetic mean as the way of averaging the price relatives (their sum divided by their number.) Actually, there are in mathematics many different forms of averaging that I might have used instead of the arithmetic mean, such as the median, the mode, the harmonic mean, the geometric mean, and others even more esoteric.

Once it is decided to use the average-of-ratios type, the next, and very significant, choice to be made is what mathematical form of averaging to use. The importance of this choice can be brought home by noting that ordinarily the index number will work out to be different numerically depending on how the ratios are averaged. The median and the mode will usually differ from each other and the rest; and the other three (counting the arithmetic mean, now) *must* differ among themselves for mathematical reasons.

As the two preceding formulas are written they are what we call "simple" index numbers. There are not explicitly different weights assigned to the different commodities and their prices in the computational process. (Sometimes these are called "unweighted" indexes. This is not a good term because it can be shown that some variants of each type implicitly and automatically allow different price quotations to weigh differently in the outcome of the calculations. To call them unweighted is misleading.)

In his classic, *The Making of Index Numbers,* Irving Fisher exhaustively examines the merits and demerits of all the simple index numbers that have ever been seriously proposed (Chapter X, "What Simple Index Number Is Best?"). The close of Chapter X reads, "At this point we are merely justified in concluding that *if* the simple weighting does not happen to be too erratic, the geometric is the best formula of the seven considered in this chapter." As I discuss shortly, we simply do not have the historical information in this study for an explicitly weighted index number. Therefore, I use the geometric index number. Fisher is my authority for this choice.

Actually, the simple geometric mean has a long lineage of approbation for what has been called the "stochastic approach to measuring changes in the value of money" (Ragnar Frisch, *Econometrica,* 1936):

W. S. Jevons (1863)
F. Y. Edgeworth (1887)
J. M. Keynes (1921)
A. L. Bowley (1926)

The reference to Keynes is in his *Treatise on Probability.* Lord Keynes maintained this position until his *Treatise on Money* (1930), when he opted for the ratio-of-aggregates type of index, provided that "actual consumption furnishes us with our standard (of weighting)." I would join Keynes in this preference, with the same proviso regarding weights. But in the current historical study no such consumption data exist.

Professor Mitchell, in his classic *The Making and Using of Index Numbers* (modestly published as Bulletin No. 656 of the U.S. Bureau of Labor Statistics in 1938), adduces three advantages of the geometric index. He is worth quoting at length.

> For the geometric mean two great merits are claimed. First, unlike the arithmetic mean, it is not in danger of distortion from the asymmetrical distribution of price fluctuations. . . . If, for example, one commodity rose tenfold in price and another commodity fell to one-tenth of the old price, the arithmetic mean would show an average rise of 505 per cent $(1,000 + 10 \div 2)$, while the geometric mean would show no change in the average, since $\sqrt{1,000 \times 10} = 100$.
>
> The second merit claimed for geometric means is that they can be shifted from one base period to another without producing results that seem to be inconsistent.
>
> A third advantage of geometric means is that they are likely to be nearer the modes of the distributions which they represent than are arithmetic means. The importance of this point will be more generally appreciated as statisticians come to study the whole array of the price fluctuations with which they deal, instead of concentrating their attention merely upon averages.

The second merit cited by Mitchell—the ability to compare with mathematical soundness index numbers at any two dates neither of which is the base—is of utmost importance in long historical researches of price such as we are engaged in here.

The Demonstration That the Lack of Explicit Weighting Is Not Serious

As mentioned in the preceding section, no information is available for weights to employ in index number calculations in the eighteenth century and earlier. To the nonstatistician this must seem a grievous, if not fatal, fault. Actually, as the practitioner of index number construction knows, the lack of weights—more properly, the use of uniform (simple) weights—is not that serious in most practice.

This was discovered by Irving Fisher by 1922 and was probably known to Wesley C. Mitchell even earlier. Fisher writes (pp. 444–445):

> The third point which strikes us in making these comparisons is how *small* is the difference made by using the careful discriminating cross weighting instead of the erratic simple weighting. This is astonishing when we consider that the two sets of weights themselves differ enormously. In the simple weighting all 36 commodities are equally important while in the cross weighting the highest weight (that for lumber was 118 times as great as the lowest (that for skins)); in 1915 the highest was 134 times the lowest; in 1916, it was 100 times; in 1917, 130 times; and in 1918, 261 times. Yet in spite of these enormous variations (and in spite of the fact that there are only 36 commodities in the list), these *unbiased* simple and cross weighted forms usually agree within five or ten per cent. In fact, out of 60 comparisons between the simple and cross weighted index numbers, there are only 13 differences that exceed five per cent and only five over ten per cent.

And later:

> Professor Wesley C. Mitchell cites many actual examples of the effect of weighting as compared to simple numbers. In general, the differences are less even than those here found. . . . Ordinarily the difference between the simple and the best weighted index number of the Aldrich Senate Report was less than three per cent.

Notice that Professor Fisher emphasizes the small differences between *unbiased* simple and weighted index numbers. The geometric that I have selected for my purpose is the best of these unbiased simple forms. It was because I knew I had to operate without weights that I chose the average-of-ratios type to start with. The unweighted ratio-of-aggregates type $\Sigma P_1/\Sigma P_0$ has a heavy inherent bias and would not do at all if it must necessarily go unweighted.

Having made this choice of index number type at the first fork in the road, I can then proceed to select the geometric average of price ratios with the full confidence of the authority of Professors Fisher and Mitchell behind me that my end results would be about the same as if I had been able to use the best weighted form with the most precise of weights applied to it.

In historical researches all errors are unwelcome, but a numerical error of the order of three to five percent is among the least of our worries.

In our present notation the formula for the simple geometric mean of the price-ratios is

$$\sqrt[N]{\pi \frac{P_1}{P_0}}$$

in which π is simply the operational symbol for multiplication, just as the earlier Σ was the operational symbol for addition.

Thus to get the *geometric* mean of a set of price-ratios you multiply them together and take the Nth root of their product (to compute their arithmetic mean you, of course, add them together and divide N into their sum).

The Comparability of Index Numbers Over Long Periods of Time

In the General Introduction to his work Lord Beveridge aptly states that ". . . whether the period chosen be short or long, price-history is a study not of isolated facts but of relations; comparison is its essence. This makes it necessary to make as sure as we can in each case that, in comparing prices at different times, we are comparing like with like." Much of the text of his Volume I is given to explaining how this comparability was sought for and preserved.

But Beveridge was dealing with the integrity of single price series. The problem is compounded when index numbers combining numerous price series are involved. This is a subject in itself, and whole sections of books on index number construction and usage have been devoted to it. One of the best treatments is by Bruce D. Mudgett, *Index Numbers,* Chapter 7, "Long-Distance and Series Comparisons." There he asks two questions: Are long-term comparisons desired? Are long-term comparisons realistic? To the first he answers "yes" and gives several examples. To the second he gives this answer:

> To the question whether these comparisons of distant situations are realistic, whether the measurements that we ultimately obtain have any counterpart in the world we live in, the answer is not so easy. In a properly qualified sense it is both yes and no, for there are some realistic features in the comparison of two widely separated periods but it is doubtful whether the limitations of such comparisons are always fully recognized."

For the reader not fully aware of these limitations a reading of Mudgett is recommended.

I would only point out that when we go so far back into price history as I do here we are like the archeologist. We nurse together the evidence that has survived with as much test of its validity as is available to us. From this partial record we try to reconstruct what the whole must have been like. Statistics, like archeology, is an inexact science when practiced on numbers that are remote and fragmentary. When we examine the prehistoric paintings of the horses in the caves at Lascaux, we probably should not complain about the pigment that was used.

But in agreement with Lord Beveridge I would say that the importance to economics and social science of having a history of prices hardly needs to be emphasized. Prices and wages are the social phenomena most susceptible to objective record over long periods of time. They reflect and measure the influence of changes in population, supply of precious metals, industrial structure and agricultural methods, trade and transport, consumption, and the technical arts. As they rise and fall the fortunes of different classes of the community are made better or worse. A comprehensive coordinated history of prices is a framework that should underlie all studies of economic development.

So much for price history. The particular point at issue here is the use of index numbers. We can find considerable justification from three passages in Joseph A. Schumpeter's *Business Cycles.*

An index of this sort may give a picture that is free from many idiosyncracies of the price movements of the individual commodities which enter into it and may be useful for many purposes. (p. 451)

This is as it should be and will not mislead, provided we confine ourselves to considering the general price level as a monetary parameter only. (p. 459)

But the old argument of practical workers that indices tend to give roughly the same picture, however well or faultily constructed, contains after all some little element of truth, which for us, it is believed, suffices to justify what we are going to do with them, provided we watch our step in drawing conclusions. (p. 460)

The foregoing discussion relates to a wholesale price index number (1560 to 1790) especially constructed for this study. No such series existed for those years. The nearest approach is to be found in E. H. Phelps Brown and S. V. Hopkins, "Seven Centuries of the Prices of Consumables, Compared with Builders' Wage-Rates," *Economica,* 1956. This was designed to approximate a cost-of-living index for workers' families and is, of course, confined to consumers' goods only. Six categories (encompassing seventeen commodities) are covered: (1) farinaceous, (2) meat, fish, (3) butter, cheese, (4) drink, (5) fuel, light, and (6) textiles. My new index number is based on a much larger sample and one intended to be more representative of wholesale prices generally. For want of anything more broadly reflective, historians have used the Phelps Brown index to measure general price movements, a purpose for which it was not intended. One of the articles I have in preparation is a detailed comparison of the behavior of the Phelps Brown–Hopkins index with my own.

Starting in 1790 there are available well-recognized index numbers at the wholesale level, so that I was not forced to carry my index further toward the present. Rather, my index is chained to the Gayer–Rostow–Schwartz index from 1790 through 1850, which in turn is spliced to the Sauerbeck-*Statist* for the interval 1850–1938, and this in turn is linked to the "Index Number of Wholesale Price" of the Central Statistical Office from 1939 through 1976. The complete series, 1560–1976, is expresed on the base 1930 = 100.0. This base was chosen because the Board of Trade once used 1930 as base 100.0 in representing prewar prices and because this was the last year preceding extraordinary gyrations in gold prices.

My original index was computed directly from the commodity price-ratios presented in the Beveridge collection, which were individually on base average 1720–1744 = 100.0. Because I used the geometric-type index number that allows any 2 nonbase years to be compared directly, it followed that I could shift the base by simple division to any other single year I chose without mathematical distortion. Thus the link-up with the Gayer–Rostow–Schwartz index was achieved in the overlap year of 1790 by the process of division. The latter index is also of the geometric type, so that the virtues of this form of index number extend homogeneously from 1560 through 1850 in the final analysis. The entire index number is given in Table 2.

Throughout this volume index numbers are stated to one decimal place. This is a convention for their easy identification as percentages and not because they are mathematically significant to one decimal.

In Appendix A is found the original Gayer–Rostow–Schwartz index number, including a description of the weighing system they used. Also to be found there is the Sauerbeck-*Statist* series in its original form. For the convenience of price historians all the other important price index numbers previously published are included which extend partly into my time-space of 1560–1790.

4 The Purchasing Power of Gold

The purchasing power of gold is, simply stated, how much it can be sold for, translated into how much can be bought with the proceeds of its sale. Therefore, variations in the purchasing power of gold can be calculated statistically by dividing the index number of gold prices year after year by the corresponding index numbers of prices of goods and services. There are refinements of logic that underlie the mathematical process, but this is what it comes down to: the index of the price of gold deflated by the index of commodity prices.

An analogy is real wages in the labor market. When we talk about real wages, we state how much can be purchased with an hour's labor. Similarly, when we talk about the purchasing power of gold (its operational wealth), we mean how much can be purchased with an ounce. This is often overlooked because we are accustomed to thinking of gold, itself, as money. It is not.

We bring together here in Chapter 4 the results of Chapter 1 and Chapter 3. The base of the gold price index number is 1930 = 100.0. The base of the wholesale commodity price index number in Chapter 3 is the same. Therefore, the base of the index of the purchasing power of gold is 1930 = 100.0. All the provisos and caveats that applied to the first two series apply to the new one which is derived from their quotients.

The index of the purchasing power of gold is presented in Table 3 and shown by years in Chart I. The purchasing power of gold is a statistical artifice, relying on the contrapuntal behavior of gold prices and commodity prices. It is a statistical expression of a market trade-off between gold and commodities.

As we review the record of Chart I, we discern that in a very interesting way the history of the purchasing power of gold divides into six periods. These are deliniated not only by the behavior of gold's purchasing power itself, but also by the type of interaction of the two other series that determine its behavior.

Years	Characteristics
1560–1700	Gold and commodity prices both rising; declining trend in gold's purchasing power.
1701–1792	Gold price stable; commodity prices fluctuating but on a horizontal trend.
1793–1821	Period of the Napoleonic Wars.
1822–1914	Gold price stable; commodity prices fluctuating but on a horizontal, long-term trend.
1915–1930	Wildly fluctuating commodity prices; gold prices responsive but in narrower ranges.
1931–1976	Soaring gold prices; commodity price revolution.

The reasons for choosing these six periods become amply clear as they are separately discussed, but they have been listed and briefly characterized at this point.

1560–1700

Overall, this was a period of rising commodity prices and rising prices of gold. Let us take as a benchmark 1570 since the commodity price index behaves quite erratically in the first 7 years.

From 1570 to 1700 gold price was steadily on the rise. Its net increase over the period was 46 percent.

The annual index of world gold production on base 1930 = 100.0 was as follows for the stated intervals:

Years	Index
1561–1600	1.1
1601–1640	1.3
1641–1680	1.4
1681–1700	1.7

Commodity prices showed temporary reverses for a year or two at a time, but their upward trend was also persistent and pronounced. The net increase over the same period was 72 percent.

The exchange rate between an ounce of gold and commodities fell appreciably and by approximately 15 percent between 1570 and 1700. (Note that for mathematical reasons this percentage change has to be calculated from the index of gold purchasing power in Table 3. It is not the simple arithmetic relation between +46 percent and +72 percent.) This was at a moderate annual rate, but it was a prolonged period during which the holders of gold, mainly the wealthy classes and the goldsmiths, saw the operational value of their holdings diminish. Gold was certainly not a hedge against inflation from 1570 to 1700.

1701–1792

During the better part of a century, gold prices were almost constant. Commodity prices showed no long-term trend upward or downward. The purchasing power of gold ended this period just about where it began.

There were, however, three distinct cycles in the commodity price level *between* the beginning and the end. From bottom to bottom these can be marked off as 1700 to 1737, 1737 to 1752, and 1752 to 1779.

With gold prices stable over 1700–1792, the three commodity price cycles generated exactly duplicating cycles in gold's purchasing power, interval by interval. The commodity price series charted against the purchasing power data show the two curves to be mirror reflections of each other, extending along a central axis representing the price of gold. In somewhat idealized form:

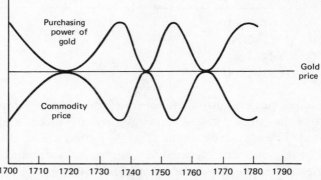

The amazing feature of these three cycles is that at the midpoints of each the three statistical series involved converged on each other at a value which all were to attain again almost *200 years later*, in 1930. To tabulate at the cyclical midpoints:

	1718	1745	1765
Purchasing power of gold	103.2	105.5	99.2
Price of gold	99.5	99.5	100.1
Commodity price index	96.4	94.3	100.9
Base year *1930*	100.0	100.0	100.0

For the three statistical series to return to mutual equality two, three, and even five decades apart (and each time at a level *all* were to show two centuries later in 1930) is a powerful attestation to the continuity of economic history.

Bearing out the theme of the title, the exchange rate between gold and commodities that held in the base year 1930 already had been achieved as early as 1650, and was realized again in 1718, 1745, and 1765, as shown in the preceding tabulation. This gold/commodity exchange rate was to hit the 1930 parity again in 1772, 1782, and 1792 in the period 1701–1792 now under review.

The persistence of this return of the commodity price index to the level of the gold index is seen again and again as the English experience is analyzed. Later it is found in the American experience as well. I call it the "Retrieval Phenomenon." Metaphorically, it is as if gold is calling commodity prices to return to it, and they always do, whether below or above for a while. (For a more complete discussion see *A Note on the Relation of Commodity Prices to Gold* at the close of Chapter 5.)

1793–1821

Wars had been fought for thousands of years but never a conflagration like the Napoleonic Wars. All Europe was involved and, through Russia, the Asiatic Dominions. Even Africa was not spared. What is more, it was the first really major conflict conducted on an international scale within a global economy resembling modern times. Banking systems were in place, paper currency with central reserves was a common medium of commerce, exchange markets were freely operative, and tradings in the precious metals had reached a sophisticated state.

For these reasons economic historians have attached much interest to the Napoleonic Wars, and I single out this period for detailed study in regard to gold and its purchasing power. The declaration of war by France in February 1793 hit England in the midst of an economic crisis of her own making. The relatively new system of country banks had overextended on a narrow reserve based mainly on deposits with the Bank of England, whose reserve of gold, in turn, was the final backup for the volume of bank notes in the country.

Prices were already rising, and by 1801 they would be up over 68 percent. Let us trace out on Chart I just what happened year by year. Considered as separate series over the period 1793–1821, the index of the price of gold and the index of commodity prices were discussed earlier in Chapters 1 and 3. Our special concern now is the purchasing power of gold.

Gold went into the Napoleonic Wars with a phenomenal record. In 1792 the index of purchasing power stood at 104.5. In only 9 years of the 132 years since 1660 had it dipped below 100.0, and even then only marginally. Purchasing power had been higher, of course. But for only 1 year in the past 55 had it gone as much as 15 percent above its 1792 level. One can well imagine that conventional wisdom of the day was that gold could certainly be trusted as a conservator of purchasing power.

If so, customary thought was in for a rude shock. Within 3 years the rate of exchange of gold for commodities had *fallen* by more than 20 percent. By 1801 it was down almost 40 percent, and the lore of gold as a haven for purchasing power must have been shattered.

As Chart I shows, there was no quick recovery from this low. As late as 1818 the index of purchasing power was hitting about 70. The chart also shows exactly why the purchasing power of gold declined. The price of gold went up. But commodity prices went up earlier, more rapidly, and further. The rate of exchange of gold for commodities swiftly declined in consequence.

The purchasing power of gold, so decimated by the Napoleonic Wars, did not regain its prewar level until 1822, and then only briefly. Not until the 1830s was it back in strength matching its prewar prowess. But it did come back.

1822–1914

By 1822 the price of gold had restabilized at its pre-Napoleonic figure of 1792, and its purchasing power was also back in place. Gold thus emerged from the Napoleonic Wars with an exchange rate for commodities the same as before, however poorly it served as a hedge against price inflation in between.

It is remarkable, and surely more than coincidental, that the *price* of gold was the same in 1821 as it was to be in 1930 with a fall never greater than 0.7 percent in between. Gold in England was to have little down-side risk in price for well over a century. What was to happen to its purchasing power is a different story.

With the price of gold practically constant, cycles in the purchasing power of gold once again became mirror images of cycles in commodity prices. This was a replay of 1700–1792, in the sense that all cycles in the purchasing power of gold were generated by fluctuations in commodity prices. But there was a striking difference in amplitude of fluctuation, and this was evidenced between 1875 and 1914.

The reader recalls that this was the "golden age" of the gold standard, and in the decline, depression, and recovery of these latter years it maintained the price of gold bullion very well.

In 1875 English commodity prices, however, went into a slide that was completely unprecedented in depth and duration. This decline, lasting for more than 20 years, carried the wholesale price level down to a point where it had not been since the early 1600s. If we take 1873 as the predepression peak, the net decline into the depth of 1896 was by 45 percent.

Also, the price depression was a long, flat-bottomed declivity. Prices were down by 35 percent as early as 1885 and stayed at or below that level until 1905. It was not until the inflation of World War I in 1915 that wholesale prices returned to their predepression level of 1875 (= 99.0). Forty years is a very long time in the history of price depressions.

The Bank of England defended the price of gold perfectly. In only 8 years did the market price average more than a pence above the Bank's buying price (stable at 3 pounds, 17 shillings, 9 pence throughout), and it never was allowed to fall below, a remarkable achievement in monetary history.

With the price of gold constant, the purchasing power of gold soared to levels never approached before. Starting with an index of 100.8 in 1875, it peaked nearly 60 percent higher in 1896. The appreciation of gold in terms of commodities had never been as high. Just as its rise was steady to that climax, its decline was far from precipitous. It tapered off gradually and did not fall back to predepression levels until 1915. Those were good days for people able to settle their accounts in gold or gold equivalents.

1915–1930

After the upward arc terminating in 1914, 1915 marked the beginning of the most precipitous drop in purchasing power in gold's history. From an index level of 113.9 in 1914, the purchasing power of gold plummeted to 50.4 in 1918, losing well over half of its commodity exchange value in 4 years. Between 1914 and 1916 alone, the drop was a drastic 37 percent. Those who believed that gold was a safe hedge against inflation were bitterly disappointed.

By 1919 gold, lagging behind commodity prices, began to move upward. It was in 1920 that England experienced its highest wholesale price level ever to date. Gold had its lowest exchange rate against commodities in four centuries of recorded history.

1931–1976

There never had been a period like this in the history of gold or commodity prices in England. The market price of gold had been very nearly stable for the 6 years preceding 1931. In 1931 England went off the gold bullion standard and the market price took off. In 4 short years it sprang upward by two-thirds. Not even the Napoleonic Wars had seen anything to match it, and Britain was not yet at war.

When England entered the war gold climbed further in price. It more than doubled in the decade following 1930 to an index of 220.7 in 1940. Heroic measures by England and her financial allies held gold steady until 1950. In that year the gold index jumped abruptly to 319.1, where it remained stable through 1967, aided partly by the formation of the London Gold Pool of eight central banks in 1961.

In 1967 the government of France removed the ban on her citizens importing gold and withdrew from the London Gold Pool. A valiant and very expensive effort by the remaining seven central banks kept the price stable through 1967. But they gave up the concerted effort in 1968, and the London price of gold quadrupled in the next 6 years.

What had happened to commodity prices in the meantime? They had come streaming down from their peak in 1920 to a low in 1933 and then bottomed out through 1935. The net decline from peak to trough was 69 percent. This was the most precipitous price decline in all of British history.

The few years from 1930 through 1933 were curious for another reason. For the first time in history, gold and commodity prices moved in opposite directions. Gold went up by 47 percent; commodity prices came down by nearly 20 percent. The conventional wisdom of the money markets required alteration.

The purchasing power of gold zoomed, of course, and increased more than 80 percent in 3 years. Nor was this to be the end of innovation for the financial world. As the Great Depression ran its course through 1935, the purchasing power of gold continued to rise to its highest level since the midsixteenth century.

Further, to underscore the dissolution of traditional values, let us note that between 1919 and 1935, in 16 years, the operational wealth of a stock of gold was increased by 287 percent, just by the owner holding fast. In those 16 short years the purchasing power of a unit of gold had gone from its lowest point to its highest point in history until then.

English price index numbers were not published during the war and an hiatus exists from 1939 through 1945. On the base 1930 = 100.0, wholesale prices in 1946 stood at 162.0. They climbed without break until they reached the end of our series at 1248.4 in 1976, a level far higher than ever before in English history, surpassing the previous record in 1920 by about 300 percent.

Since January 1975 the price of gold has fallen drastically. For a second time in a generation we have seen gold prices and commodity prices move in opposite directions, with the further twist that this time, unlike the 1930s, gold prices have declined while commodity prices have soared.

5 The Purchasing Power of Gold in Inflation and Deflation

In Chapter 4 we followed the purchasing power of gold chronologically straight through from 1560 to 1976. Periods of price inflation and deflation were encountered, along with substantial intervals of price stability. All these periods of inflation, deflation, and stability were treated in sequence as they developed a linear history of gold's purchasing power.

Now let us go back and collect the separate episodes of price inflation to find if there are any generalities that attach to these, and similarly to gather for special analysis all the periods of price deflation. In short, I divide price history in England into periods of inflation and deflation.

There is no common agreement on the definitions of the terms "inflation" and "deflation," indeed, some authorities assign them different contexts. Some present-day writers use them simply as descriptive terms for periods of rapidly rising or falling prices; others confine them to a description of monetary phenomena underlying price behavior (see, e.g., J. A. Schumpeter, *Business Cycles,* pp. 260–262).

In this book I use "inflation" and "deflation" in a sense descriptive of prices' behavior. Inflation refers to a period of rapidly rising prices; deflation connotes an interval of swiftly falling prices.

Even when this choice of nomenclature is adopted, another arbitrary, that is, subjective, element enters into the semantics: how fast is rapid; how precipitous is swift? Also, this open question has to be related to the length of the time period which is descriptively designated as inflationary or deflationary.

Since I cannot hope to argue my way through to any common agreement on such subjective matter, I simply adopt an arbitrary schema and state my considered selection of terminal dates for periods of inflation and deflation in English price history. The reader can examine the same charts and tables that I do and either agree with my choice or make a choice of his own. In the latter event he also can use my basic tables to rework my analyses to suit time segments of his own choosing.

With all the *caveats* just expressed I would select from a reading of Chart I the following episodes of price history:

Inflationary	Deflationary
1623–1658	1658–1669
1675–1695	
1702–1723	1723–1738
1752–1776	
1792–1813	1813–1851
1897–1920	1873–1896
1934–1976	1920–1933

We must be careful not to infer from these episodes of inflation and deflation movements in trade approximating what we now refer to as business cycles. Regarding the earlier years Wesley C. Mitchell argues cogently that this modern-day phenomenon did not appear until the advent of a "money-making" economy and explains:

> To repeat: we do not say that a business economy has developed in any community until most of its economic activities have taken the form of making and spending money. That way of arranging production, distribution and consumption is the matter of importance—not the use of money as a medium of exchange (*Business Cycles, the Problem and Its Setting,* 1927, p. 63).

Mitchell agrees with Mentor Bouniatian that no business cycle of a modern type can be found before the close of the eighteenth century (Bouniatian, *Geschichte der Handelskrisen in England, 1640–1840*).

There were, of course, bad times and good as long as economic history has been set down. These spells of adversity and prosperity go back as far as events have been systematically recorded, and the records of Egyptians, Romans and Greeks are replete with them. But until the turn into the nineteenth century these events were largely accounted for by crop failures, epidemics, wars, civil disorders, political struggles, and deviant public finance (including chicanery) in respect to crises and depression, and by good harvests, prolonged peace, enlightened rule, and sound recoinage on the side of revival and prosperity. It was not until the uses of money in economic dealings reached a fairly advanced stage that economic vicissitudes and well-being took on the undulating character of a business cycle.

These are meant as remarks on the forms of the economic disturbance and not necessarily on their severity. Indeed, living may have been more precarious and economic fortunes more capricious in medieval towns than in more modern cities. But it was not until a large part of the populace was receiving and spending money incomes, producing goods for large markets, organizing enterprises with few employers and many employees, and using credit instruments in support of all this that economic fluctuations took on the character of business cycles.

It is no accident of scholarship that the first treatise on the business cycle was published in 1819—*Nouveaux Principes d'Économic Politique* by J. C. L. Simonde de Sismondi. The period was one of economic distress. As Napoleon's eventual fall became imminent, English producers and merchants accumulated large inventories for export in anticipation of reopened continental markets. Waterloo was followed by several months of brisk trade and attendant optimism. But it soon became apparent that Europeans lacked the money to support the boom. Heavy inventories of English goods overbalanced the markets, and many firms went bankrupt. Some recovery followed thereafter, and 1818 showed favorable business activity, but 1819 was again severely depressed.

Sismondi, who had been influenced by Adam Smith, was impressed by the economic disarray he saw around him. He wrote:

> I was deeply affected by the commercial crisis which Europe had experienced of late, by the cruel sufferings of the industrial workers which I had witnessed in Italy, Switzerland and France and which all reports showed to have been at least as severe in England, in Germany and in Belgium.

Sismondi was particularly puzzled by the English experience. If the country where economic liberty had freest practical expression—the country where the new methods of machine production had their greatest advance—could be plunged into depression by the return of peace, then something must be wrong with the system of economic *laissez faire*. Sismondi set himself to find out what it was, and his *Nouveaux Principes* became the first study of the business cycle as such.

This digression occurred while explaining that in the earlier periods of our study we must not necessarily associate prolonged price movements with cycles of prosperity and depression in the modern sense. At the other end of the chronology there is, at this writing, a severe recession in the United Kingdom accompanied by marked inflation of prices. Again, there is no necessary statistical correlation between inflation and prosperity.

Nonetheless, it is important to know what was happening during each of the designated periods of price movements to understand the relationships between commodity prices and gold. Therefore, the subsequent discussion is organized in terms of these periods, and a brief historical account of what was happening in each of them is given.

Fortunately, for an understanding of events in the earlier periods, we have a fascinating account by William R. Scott drawn from his detailed study of British business records in manuscripts, official reports, books, pamphlets, and newspapers from the middle of the sixteenth century to 1720 (*The Constitution and Finance of English, Scottish and Irish Joint-Stock Companies to 1720*, 1972). One shortcoming of the Scott record, however, is that he was most interested in what he called "crisis," and disproportionate attention was given to bad times. For the later years I have drawn on our general knowledge of events but have relied heavily on Sir John Clapham's 3-volume work, *An Economic History of Modern Britain* (1951), and his 2-volume *The Bank of England* (1944). Feavearyear's *The Pound Sterling* is useful throughout.

I must emphasize that the narrative which accompanies each period in no way purports to give an explanation of causes of price behavior or the purchasing power of precious metals. The purpose is solely to orient the reader toward events that were taking place. At the opening of each narrative is a statistical statement of the length of the period, the change in commodity prices, and the change in the purchasing power of gold. These percentage changes are derived (as they must be) from the original respective indexes computed on the base 1930 = 100.0, to be found in Tables 2 and 3.

A very beneficial effect, incidentally, comes from considering these index changes period by period. Over intervals of 20 or 30 years the composition of the sample of prices remains much

more nearly the same than when comparisons are made over
centuries. And, what is equally important, the *quality* of each
good remains much more nearly the same. Hence we are on
much firmer ground in short-term comparisons of index numbers than in the very long comparisons sometimes involved
elsewhere in this volume.

One final word of introduction. We are not concerned with a
transient swing of short duration upward or downward in
prices, but rather with fundamental changes in price levels of
substantial duration. Fortunately, the reader with curiosity can
look up the particular events that might interest him and see
from the tables and charts what happened to prices and purchasing power on those occasions. (If you are interested in the
effects of the collapse of the South Sea Bubble, look up 1720.)

1623–1658: INFLATIONARY; 35 YEARS

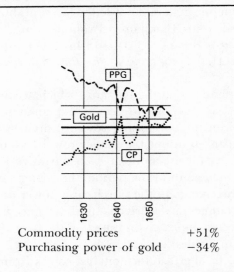

Commodity prices   +51%
Purchasing power of gold   −34%

From 1610 to 1630 the English Mint was nearly inactive in silver
(Sir John Craig, *The Mint*, p. 415). The coins that continued in

active circulation grew worse and worse, so that trading prices for commodities by tale might have been expected to increase sharply.

Spanish treasure from Mexico came to have an effect on English prices in an interesting way. By 1630 Spain was fighting a religious war against Protestantism in most of Europe while at the same time trying to maintain her administrative and political influence in the Low Countries. Her internal finances were desperate. She could pay the costs of administering The Netherlands only with the silver that came from Mexico. This silver could not be shipped directly to The Netherlands. To get it across the Atlantic was dangerous enough; to send it up the English Channel was suicidal.

In 1630 James I made peace with Spain, and in the treaty an agreement was made of the utmost importance to England's economy. This agreement provided that all the silver needed by Spain for financing her operations in the Low Countries should be brought to England in English ships. At least a third of this would be coined in England, being paid for with bills drawn on Antwerp, and the remainder either disposed of in like manner in England in exchange for Flemish money or shipped directly on to Flanders. The advantage to Spain lay in the greater safety for its bullion. The Dutch, Spain's bitter enemy at this stage, would hesitate to attack the well-armed English vessels. Spain would ultimately receive in The Netherlands the wherewithal to pay its bills.

The plan worked well for many years. The merchants of Madrid also fell in with the scheme to transfer effectively their funds to the Low Countries when needed. The influx of silver for England was momentous. Some accounts suggest that 10 million pounds' worth of Spanish silver was coined at the Mint between 1630 and 1643. In any case, the total coinage of silver in the rein of Charles I (1625–1649) was more than 8¾ millions, which was about twice the amount of silver coined during the whole of Elizabeth's reign (1558–1603), including her great recoinage.

The Monopolies Act of 1624 is of great importance in this period. In allowing a monopoly for inventions for a stated number of years it has been called the first patent law. It may very well have set the base for England's later technical progress.

Companies, whether chartered, joint-stock, regulated, or informal, were not usually prosperous between 1625 and 1645, and some had rough going indeed between 1645 and 1660. Because of the prospect of failures the concept of limited liability of shareholders had its inception during this period.

The troubles of the forties were not favorable to foreign trade or to company promotions. But there was one group that insecurity favored—the goldsmiths. William R. Scott, *Constitution and Finance*, lists for this period:

1620–1625   Effects of crisis in cloth trade, Dutch competition in foreign trade; default of East India and Russia companies; bad harvests; plague; deaths in London, 35,403.

1630   Famine; townage dispute; plague; deaths in London, 1317.

1636–1637   Depression through the monopolies of Charles I; plague; deaths in London, 10,400.

1640   Seizure of bullion by Charles I. [Note: this was particularly disturbing to trade because the king blocked about 120,000 pounds worth of silver bullion in the Mint belonging to merchants of Madrid and ordered that nothing be paid out on it. English merchants were aghast at this cavalier treatment of their kind. The incident was long taken as proving how unsafe a national bank would be under a monarchy.]

1646–1649   Exhaustion of the country through Civil War; great dearth; high taxation.

1652–1654   Losses of shipping in the Dutch War; possibly, too, effects of the Navigation Act.

1658–1669: DEFLATIONARY; 11 YEARS

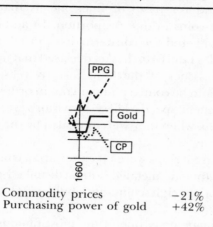

Commodity prices   −21%
Purchasing power of gold   +42%

Charles II (1660–1685) took several major steps toward putting England on a purely automatic monetary standard. Thomas Mun's immensely influential *England's Treasure by Foreign Trade* was published in 1664, although he had been advocating its principal thesis—the removal of all restrictions on the export of bullion—in powerful circles before. By the earlier years of his reign Charles II was freely granting licenses to export bullion. In 1663 Parliament passed a comprehensive statute entitled "An Act for Encouragement of Trade." One important provision was for free export of any kind of foreign coin or gold or silver bullion.

It was also under Charles II in 1663 that the new machine of the Frenchman Blondeau was installed, and for the first time coins with milled edges were issued from the Mint. The coin clipper (a prime mover in coinage debasement) had at last been circumvented.

Heavy pressure grew in these times from both merchants and goldsmiths—each with different motives—for Mint charges to be abolished on new coinage. In 1666 an Act was passed providing that any person bringing bullion to the Mint could have it assayed, melted, and coined. Further, for every pound weight of standard metal he should receive a pound weight of coins without charge, and for bases of finer metals than standard he should receive coins in due proportion. In addition, for those who still remembered the consternation caused by the blocking action of Charles I in 1640, the Act declared that no "stop" should be put on the issues of the Mint for any reason—that metal brought in should be coined and paid out in order of receipt and with all convenient speed. These provisions were to remain in force until 1925, when they were repealed by the Gold Standard Act of that year.

Thus three great steps were taken toward a completely decontrolled and automatic metallic standard: milled edges of coins, free export of foreign coins and bullion, abolition of Mint charges.

As a numismatic note, one of the most famous coins in commerce came into being in this period. A royal warrant in 1663 required the Mint to stamp all coins issued using bullion brought to it by the African Company with a tiny elephant, the trademark of the company. This was a favor given as an advertisement, but it caught the public fancy and the famous "guinea piece" was born.

Returning to the work of William R. Scott we find listed for this period:

1659–1660   Losses in Spanish War, especially in cloth trade, strain of continued high taxation.

1664–1667   Dutch War, plague (deaths 68,596), Great Fire, Dutch fleet in the Thames, 1667. Run on bankers.

1675–1695: INFLATIONARY; 20 YEARS

The first credit inflation began in this period. But to understand it we must go back to earlier years and the founding of the practice of banking in England.

| Commodity prices | +27% |
| Purchasing power of gold | −21% |

As mentioned earlier the treaty with Spain in 1630 brought about a vast influx of silver bullion to be coined. This enormous mass of full-weight new coins was thrown in with the existing debased coinage, some of it left over even from Elizabethan times. With the good new coins mixed indiscriminately with the light coins already in circulation, there was money to be made. The astute goldsmiths stepped in to make it.

They solicited from merchants and brokers cash for safekeeping for short periods and even overnight. For this they would sometimes pay the owners 2 and 3 percent. What the owners did not know was that the goldsmiths had staffs who would sift out the good coins left in their care, replace them with light, and return the light coins only.

In a description by a traveler from Amsterdam:

It is the goldsmiths, especially those on Lombard St., who are the greatest merchants and London cashiers, and who will receive any man's money for nothing, and pay it for them the same or the next day, and meantime keep people in their upper rooms to cull and weigh all they receive, and melt down the weighty and transport it to foreign parts.

Here was the beginning of banking in England. (There was nothing uniquely nefarious about it; the Dutch had started the practice half a century earlier.)

During the Civil War and the disturbances of Cromwell landowners and merchants often transferred their liquid funds to the goldsmiths for safekeeping. The goldsmiths were ready to pay interest, for reasons just disclosed. They were soon to find fresh uses for these deposits once the heavy coins had been removed for melting. Small sums were privately borrowed at interest from goldsmiths as early as 1650. But this new business only really began to boom when the government started to borrow.

By 1675 the smaller elements of the profession were involved in the action, and Macaulay writes of their agents haunting the arcades of the Royal Exchange and soliciting the merchants, with profound bows, to keep their cash.

From this time on, the system of credit and credit currency was developing. The first bank note probably evolved in the following fashion. You made a deposit of cash with a goldsmith, an account was opened in your name, and you were given a receipt stating the interest you were to get and the length of notice you must give before withdrawal. At first these were simply treated as deposit receipts of the modern kind. As early as 1668 we know, however, from Pepys' *Diary*, that they had become negotiable. Soon after that date we find references to them as "cash notes" or "bills."

Now we come to our inflationary period, opening in 1675. The seventeenth century saw the several advances toward a free metallic standard under Charles II which we noted earlier. But now there was a new kind of currency made of paper and promises. The problem of freeing the coinage was to be overshadowed by the problem of controlling the paper. And trouble was to come very soon.

The famous "stoppage" of the Exchequer occurred on January 2, 1672. This meant that the government stopped paying its old bills and used all new tax receipts to pay for new orders. The new war with Holland was the reason. The stoppage reaffirmed to the commercial world that a national bank would be unsafe in the clutches of a monarchy and assured that when a central bank came (in 1694) it would be put in private hands.

In the prosperous years following the stoppage a new breed of goldsmith—bankers—grew up. They stayed out of state affairs and did not get burned again by letting a king be one of their debtors. The bulk of their funds was applied to supporting the rapidly growing commerce based upon London.

Although Charles II had earlier shocked the financial world with indebtedness and stoppages, the last 6 years of his reign until 1685 were a period of rectitude, economy, and debt reduction. Credit had improved sufficiently by this time that in London all payments of size were made with paper money. Every merchant had his account with a banker. The position of credit currency in the nation's economy was completely established.

Now a surprising but possibly predictable operation got under way. The milled edge on a coin defeated the clipper, but it assured a melter that a good coin had fallen into his hands. It is not too much to say that as soon as the Mint issued the heavy milled coins they were taken out of circulation and melted down for their bullion.

The position of the Mint was ludicrous. Sir Dudley North regarded it as "a perpetual motion found out, whereby to coin and melt without ceasing, and so feed goldsmiths and coiners at the public charge" (Discourses on Trade, 1691). John Locke, our philosopher-cum-financier agreed with him and said so in Some Considerations of the Consequences of the Lowering of Interest and Raising the Value of Money (1692, p. 147). It was even said by William Lowndes at the time that the workmen in the Mint were making copies of old clipped and hammered coins and issuing them to get out some coinage that would stay in circulation (and probably make a profit for themselves). By 1695 it was estimated by Lowndes, then Secretary of the Treasury, that milled silver formed only one-half percent of the coinage in circulation.

War with France broke out in 1689. There would have been grave financial difficulties even with a sound coinage. When the Exchequer stopped payments in 1672 its debts amounted in pounds to 2¼ million, and annual revenue was about 1.6. King William III by 1694 was spending 2½ million a year on the Army alone and by 1697 had piled up debts amounting to over 20 million.

William, who acceded to the throne in 1689, used almost every device then known for raising money and invented a few. He and his government raised taxes as far as they dared. They borrowed on personal loans from everyone who would lend. They issued a lottery loan of a million pounds, with large prizes for lucky numbers in addition to 10 percent on the principal invested in a lottery. Finally, and almost as an afterthought, they founded the Bank of England.

(There is much special literature on the Bank of England, and it is not our present purpose to go into the subject deeply, since we are concerned with its effects only on price phenomena. Those wishing more should see, in addition to J. H. Clapham, *The Bank of England;* Michael Godfrey, *A Short Account of the Bank of England;* and Thorold Rogers, *The First Nine Years of the Bank of England*, among others.)

The Ways and Means Act of May 1694 gave the Bank its charter. It was to lend the government 1,200,000 pounds at 8 percent, a moderate rate considering the state of the government's credit at that time. The Bank was to receive in return the considerable privilege of incorporating a joint-stock company.

It was perfectly clear from the onset that the new institution would do a regular banking business—that it should be in the position of receiving deposits and creating a credit currency; it was not created solely for the purpose of bailing out the government. It is more than a distinction of form to remember that the Bank as an institution loaned the money to the King, and not the subscribers of the Bank collectively. Most of them individually would not have been attracted to loan to the King for a mere 8 percent, at the time. What attracted the subscriber was the opportunity to get into the first joint-stock bank in England—a venture with extraordinary promise of profitability for a long time to come.

The Bank from the beginning was a bank of issue and not merely deposit. One of its first acts was inflation of credit of the simplest, most direct kind. The entire issue of capital of the Bank of 1,200,000 pounds was quickly subscribed, but only 720,000 pounds was actually put up. As soon as it was clear that the subscription would be successful, preparation was made for printing notes. All 1,200,000 pounds were soon paid out to the government in bank bills with the seal of the Bank ("sealed bills"). These were quickly paid out by the government throughout the country and accepted at par. As Michael Godfrey, first Deputy Governor of the Bank of England so innocently said, "The Bank have called in but £720,000. . . They have paid into the Exchequer the whole of the £1,200,000. . . . The rest is left to circulate in trade" (*A Short Account*, p. 3). Godfrey foresaw no ill effects, but commodity prices were to feel them very soon. England was still a thin domestic economy.

The original Act establishing the Bank contained the wording ". . . they shall not owe at any one time more than the said sum (£1,200,000)," so of course when its issue of "sealed" bills had reached this sum it raised the question whether it could issue any more. The Court decided that once this limit had been reached, new sealed bills could be issued only to replace those that came in. Curiously enough, it held that the ruling applied only to sealed bills and not at all to the less formal "running cash notes" which did not bear the seal of the bank and an engraving of Britannia sitting on a pile of money. Instead, the "running cash notes" were signed by the Cashier.

These notes were soon issued freely and accepted unquestioningly. Somewhat prophetically they were nicknamed "Speed's Notes," but that was really because Speed was the surname of the Cashier of the Bank of England. As early as August 1694 a million pounds' worth had been issued for the Army alone, and that was only the beginning.

The financial strain of the government had been greatly relieved. Some of this came from lottery money, some from taxation, but much of it had been made possible by the first credit inflation in the history of Britain.

The decade closing this period were boom years. It was a time of great ferment in Britain, artistically, financially, and technically. St. Paul's was built; the Royal Society founded; the Hudson Bay Company came into its greatest prosperity. Domestic industrial activity was marked by the formation of companies for numerous and varied ventures: leather, saltpetre, pumping machines, wallpaper, printing paper, plate and bottle glass, saw-milling, water supply, various kinds of munitions—a very long list. All this had been much encouraged by official acts supporting infant industries in 1681. In total the number of companies in Britain rose from 22 in 1688 to nearly 150 by 1695.

Perhaps the most important aspect of commercial progress in the second half of the seventeenth century was the burgeoning of trade with the East. The East India Company, though founded at the turn of the century, was now paying off most handsomely. The company, whose capital was 370,000 pounds at the outset, paid a bonus of 100 percent in 1676. The value of all imports from India increased by thirty times in the reign of the last two Stuarts, 1660–1688.

Scott's chronology gives the following for this period, starting with an entry for 1672 and closing with an entry for 1696–1697, both of which seem relevant:

1672   Stop of the Exchequer, failure of banker.

1678   Prohibition of trade with France, expectation of war with Holland, run on bankers.

1682   Run on bankers occasioned by state of home politics, foreign trade little affected.

1686   Depression in cloth trade, failure of Corporation bank (1685, on news of Monmouth's rebellion), foreign trade still fairly prosperous.

1688   Revolution—run on bankers.

1696–1697   The financial strain of the war, exaggerated ideas of the nature of credit, bad harvests, suspension of cash payments by Bank of England, failure of Land bank schemes.

1702–1723: INFLATIONARY; 21 YEARS

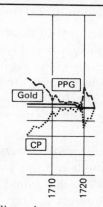

| Commodity prices | +25% |
| Purchasing power of gold | −22% |

Only the abrupt reversal between 1695 and 1702 leads me to consider this period as a separate inflationary episode for narrative purposes. Otherwise, the reader might wish to think of a general swelling of inflation from 1675 through 1723. In this case the data would look as follows:

| Commodity prices | +37% |
| Purchasing power of gold | −23% |

This was a period during which the role of the new Bank of England (founded in 1694) began to have its lasting effects on commerce and finance. Earlier its function had been largely to finance the war and its fiscal aftermath.

The progress of credit currency was substantial during these years. Although this credit currency took many forms, and some of it was quite informal, the following principal instruments can be identified:

1. Engraved and watermarked private bank notes were developed. Because they were harder to forge, hence safer, they began to supercede both the written note and the customer's draft on his banker. Safety and acceptability breed usage, so credit circulation in this form increased.

2. Still the most common form of paper money in this period was the banker's promissory note to his client, made out as a printed form and payable either on demand, or following a specified date, to whomever was the bearer at the time. So-called "bearers' notes," having the advantage of anonymity of payee, were, therefore, convenient—and convenience breeds usage.

3. One of the more curious credit currencies was the malt ticket. A tax on malt was voted, and the government immediately issued to the public tickets that would later be paid out of tax collections, bearing interest in the meantime. The tickets passed from person to person as currency, and, while current, added to the money supply without a corresponding contraction elsewhere. In fact, government lottery tickets passed as currency in the same way between time of ticket sale and time of lottery.

4. Exchequer bills became a regular method of raising short-term loans. They were made out payable on demand by the Bank of England and passed as freely as Bank of England notes, a mainstay of credit currency of the time.

These several forms of paper money came into play during this inflationary period (1702–1723) but were confined to large transactions. Coins remained the principal media for common transactions on the streets.

The composition of the coinage was, however, undergoing a

great shift from earlier times. A calculation from the Mint figures shows that between 1700 and 1725 the coinage was

Gold	£ 11,452,000
Silver	£ 557,000

In the preceding 25 years gold and silver coinage had been almost equal at 7.5 million each.

England had gone on the gold standard effectively in 1717 with the proclamation forbidding the paying or receiving of guineas at higher than 21 shillings.

These facts are worth bearing in mind, for there are still those who say that gold was not important to England until 1816, when the Liverpool Act placed her on the gold standard by legislative action for the first time.

Another feature that marked this period of prosperity was the rapid increase in joint-stock companies and the pooling of financial resources which they made possible. According to Scott, in 1695 there were 140 such companies with a capital of 4.5 million pounds, whereas total capitalization rose to nearly 21 million by 1717. By all evidence the expansion of this form of business organization continued to rise rapidly.

The importance of this kind of organization to industrial development can hardly be overestimated, because it allowed for both the pooling of the resources of small operators who could not undertake the entrepreneurial role alone, and the sharing of risk that it allowed.

There were dangers of excess in the form of highly speculative ventures, some of which went broke. The mania of 1719–1720 is an example of this. Also the promotion of companies provided a channel through which funds could flow away from, rather than toward, productive purposes.

For perspective it is well to remember that England was still a thin economy during this period. At the time of Queen Anne (1702–1714) a contemporary estimated that the metropolitan area of London, the more or less continuous town, and going well beyond the City, had about half a million population. London was at least fourteen times the size of the next biggest town and accounted for approximately one-twelfth the entire population of England and Wales (Sir John Clapham, *A Concise Economic History of Britain,* p. 189). If this is correct the total population was of the order of 6 million only—a population economically, socially, and politically dominated by one huge town in the south.

W. R. Scott had gleaned these doleful events from the archives:

1701	Tension between East India companies, political situation, run on banks, and consequent failures.
1704–1708	Losses in the war, financial strain, tensions between England and Scotland, fears of a French invasion, run on Bank of England.
1710–1711	Financial strain of the war, change of ministry.
1714	Fears of the consequences of the succession, reported death of Anne, run on the Bank of England.
1715	Rebellion.
1718	Fears of an invasion.
1720	Panic follows the collapse of speculation (South Sea Bubble). [Note: the last stands out clearly in Chart I and registers a fall of 17% in the price index in one year.]

1752–1776: INFLATIONARY; 24 YEARS

The Industrial Revolution probably has been dissected and discussed by economic historians more than any other occurrence in British history. Various dates have been suggested for its beginning, but with a phenomenon so amorphous it is impossible to

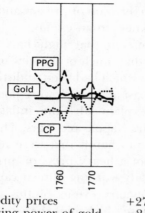

Commodity prices	+27%
Purchasing power of gold	−21%

achieve unanimity on when it began. There is, however, some-thing of a consensus that it had its immediate antecedents in the latter half of the eighteenth century. We may take it that this inflationary period (1752–1776) was associated with the early rise of the Industrial Revolution.

Insofar as this linkage of inflation existed it was a demand-pull rather than a cost-push relationship. Industrial growth at this time was aimed toward the supply of goods at medium and low prices and in large quantity. It was not intended to serve the wealthy few, but rather the large markets of the increasing population.

In 1750 England was already distinguished among its Euro-pean counterparts for the variety and prosperity of its industry.

Also helpful to the moderation of inflation was the healthy state of her farming technology. Farming played an important part in ongoing industrialization by providing an adequate sup-ply of food without recourse to expensive imports, and by set-ting labor free for employment in towns.

The evidence is that the population was increasing rapidly at this time. Admittedly, the evidence is inferential because the first national census was not taken until 1801. Curiously enough, one was proposed in 1753 but rejected by Parliament on the ground that it would be an invasion of privacy and dangerous because it might reveal weakness to an enemy.

Another phenomenon that might have relevance to the form of this inflation is that much of the new industrial development went on in districts which had been undistinguished as industrial producers in the past and which were poor and backward. This would serve to explain why the inflation was smooth and gradual up until the Napoleonic Wars. The wage payments were widely dispersed into hands that were not prosperous before. Also, there was not a heavy press on productive facilities and labor supply, already working at near capacity.

The purely monetary events of this period have been described earlier. Those which might be associated with the inflation of commodity prices are

1. The state of the debased coinage of the time, which would tend to increase the prices demanded in coins;
2. The rapid development of the country banks and the attendant increase in credit instruments.

The financial crises of 1763, 1772, and 1775 also should be noted.

Another factor that may surprise those not familiar with British history is that during the 50 years following 1760 she was at war more than half the time. In addition to the material demands this placed on her, England was persistently meeting the direct or delayed costs of financing warfare, often with deficit financing.

Although this period is dominated by the upsweep of the industrial revolution, some singular events should be noted. There was a boom followed by a collapse associated with the Seven Year's War ending in 1763. A short depression and a rapid revival continued to 1772, when the failure of an important banking house caused a severe panic, the worst since the bursting of the South Sea Bubble. The war with the American colonies, which closed this period, actually caused a depression in trade. An excited boom followed the end of the war but collapsed in 1783 with a financial panic.

1792–1813: INFLATIONARY; 21 YEARS

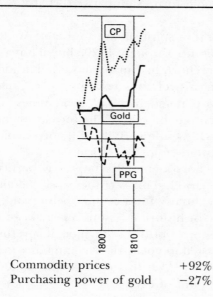

| Commodity prices | +92% |
| Purchasing power of gold | −27% |

The development of heavy industry was an especially prominent feature of British industrial activity after 1780. It became a true revolution of industry because it was marked by sudden and momentous innovations linked with names of individuals. (This is far too extensive a phenomenon to describe here, but for the reader who is interested a good volume to consult is P. Mantoux, *The Industrial Revolution in the Eighteenth Century*, New York, 1928.)

It is now convenient to remind the reader that we engaged upon these commentaries not to explain periods of inflation and deflation but rather to appreciate the events occurring during such periods.

The task can now be eased by having recourse to an unusual volume by Willard Long Thorp published by the National Bureau of Economic Research in 1926, entitled *Business Annals*. In it he gleaned year-by-year the publications bearing on business and financial activities in the major countries of the world and, almost in note form, summarized what was happening in each of them.

Thorp's book is in spirit similar to that of W. R. Scott which was used earlier up through 1720, but Thorp's book is far superior in that Thorp had many more publications to consult (since the business press was enlarging over time) and, more important, Thorp noted bad *and* good times, whereas Scott tended to concentrate on crises. The format for England in the period 1792–1813 is to give Willard Thorp's commentaries in modified, sometimes amplified, form.

The use of Thorp's annual synopses is particularly appropriate for this period. This was the most chaotic time in England's economic history for a century before and after and one often looked to for historical lessons on what can happen when most of the Western world is in turmoil. Therefore, the reader especially interested in gold prices, commodity prices, and purchasing power may wish to follow in the tables and chart a year-by-year account of events.

Before getting into a detailed account, it is good to remember that this was generally a period of major wartime activity— preparation as well as combat. Also, it was a period of mismanagement—or complete lack of management—of the paper currency, because England for the first time did not back her paper with specie.

Thorp's *Annals* give the following synposes:

1792. Prosperity; financial strain.

Continued prosperity and expansion in trade; speculation; imports decline but exports increase strongly.

Easy money tightens in autumn; security prices high.

Crop failure with higher price.

Mobilization of forces in preparation for war, December.

1793. Recession; panic; depression.

Slackening of activity to stagnation, spring; many failures, especially second quarter; commodity prices advance sharply and peak, spring, and then decline; reduction in foreign trade, chiefly exports.

Very tight money eases, summer; panic, February to July, with runs on banks and failures; government relieves situation by issuing Exchequer bills.

Moderate crop.

War with France declared, February; France seizes all British goods, October, and England issues severe navigation restrictions; English army lands in Flanders, but is driven from Toulon; civil unrest causes suspension of Habeas Corpus Act.

1794. Depression.

Industry at a standstill; cotton trade most severely hit; revival in foreign trade.

Money easy.

Deficient crop and rising prices.

English victories at sea and defeats on land.

1795. Revival.

Some improvement in industry; rapid rise in commodity prices; foreign trade dull.

Easy money tightens, last half-year; foreign exchange unfavorable.

Deficient crop and very high prices.

Military impressment results in civil unrest, summer.

1796. Uneven prosperity.

Industrial activity; slow rise in commodity prices; foreign trade advances to new high record.

Continued tightening in money market; gold scarcity; security values decline.

Abundant harvest.

Severe distress, first half-year; extension of scope of poor relief; French invasion of Ireland fails, December.

1797. Recession; panic; depression.

Activity yields to stagnation, spring; unemployment; slight decline in commodity prices, summer; many failures; foreign trade reduced.

Monetary stringency; panic, February, with runs on banks; Bank of England suspends specie payments, February.

Poor crop, fair price.

Army and Navy mutinies; British allies make separate peace with France.

1798. Depression.

Dullness in industry; revival in export trade.

Money eases; unfavorable foreign exchange and large imports of bullion.

Good crop, low price.

French invasion of England threatened, February; Irish rebellion, May; naval successes; Pitt presents income tax, December.

1799. Depression.

Inactivity continues; after feverish speculation, prices of imported goods collapse; decline in imports, active exports.

Money tightens; improvement in security prices.

Harvest very deficient, especially wheat; prices very high.

Great distress and riots; trade unionism checked by passing of Combination Act.

1800. Depression.

Continued stagnation of industry; further rise in commodity prices, especially foodstuffs; active foreign trade.

Money eases.

Harvest failure; very high prices; duties on grain suspended and active importation.

Distress and riots; further extension of Combination Act.

1801. Depression; revival.

Improvement in industry late in year; commodity prices rise rapidly to peak, second quarter, and then decline; commerce prosperous.

Money easy; rapid depreciation of currency.

Moderate harvest.

Peace of Amiens with France, October.

1802. Prosperity.

Rapid improvement and expansion in industry; building brisk; speculation; commodity price decline checked, last half-year; larger exports.

Money easy; large gold premium.

Treaty of Amiens, March; income tax repealed.

1803. Prosperity; recession; depression.

With breaking of peace, industry slackens and commerce becomes stagnant; commodity prices rise to peak, third quarter; many failures.

Money tightens; gold premium greatly reduced.

Moderate harvest.

Peace broken, May, and troops mustered, June; embargo declared on all French and Dutch ships, May; Emmet's rebellion in Ireland, July; income tax reestablished; war in India.

1804. Mild depression.

Industry quiet, activity being concentrated on amassing of war forces; foreign trade dull.

Money eases.

Very deficient wheat and barley crops; sudden and great rise of prices following passage of new corn law with higher duties.

Spain declares war, December; French ports blockaded.

1805. Revival.

Improvement in industry and trade; slight rise in commodity prices.

Money easy.

Average crop.

Alliance with Russia formed, April; Austria, Sweden, and Naples join coalition against France, September; French and Spanish fleets defeated at Trafalgar, October; severe defeats of Austrians and Russians, December.

1806. Prosperity.

General activity in industry; commodity prices decline; decreased imports and increased exports.

Money fairly easy.

Moderate harvests, lower prices.

Prussian ports closed to British shipping, March; Napoleon's Berlin Decree establishes "Continental System," November.

1807. Recession.

Activity continues, though slackening; commodity prices decline further; increased failures; many new companies and active speculation; marked reduction in foreign trade.

Money eases.

Poor harvest, lower prices.

Slave trade abolished, February; active war in Spain begun; expedition to Constantinople and Egypt fails; Treaty of Tilsit creates coalition of all European nations against England, July; American embargo declared, December; Napoleon extends blockade by Milan Decree, December.

1808. Mild depression.

Stagnation in manufacturing and further reduction in foreign trade; commodity prices rise rapidly; speculation; joint-stock companies boom, enormous exports to South America.

Easy money tightens; security market very active.

Military successes in Portugal.

1809. Revival; prosperity.

Improvement in industry; prices high and speculation frenzied; extraordinary increase in foreign trade.

Money market tightens; increased gold premium.

Poor crop, very high prices.

America passes Non-Intercourse Act.

1810. Prosperity; recession.

Activity and speculation continue to crisis, July; wild price fluctuations give way to general decline; many failures; manufacturing paralysis and unemployment, autumn; record imports with little increase in exports.

Money very tight; bank failures, summer; gold advances and large premiums.

Good wheat and oats crops, fair barley; high prices.

Military successes in Portugal.

1811. Deep depression.

Complete stagnation of industry; many failures; unemployment; wage cuts; commodity prices decline; marked reduction in foreign trade.

Money eases; Exchequer bills issued; currency improves.

Deficient crops; very high prices.

Universal distress; Luddite riots; war successes after April; Regent appointed to displace George III, November.

1812.   Revival.

Gradual improvement in industry despite unrest in manufacturing districts; distress and unemployment in cotton industry; revival of speculation, autumn; sharp rise in commodity prices; many failures; recovery of export trade.

Money easy; increased gold premium.

Fair crops; very high prices.

Severe distress, riots; war with United States declared, June; victories in Spain; Napoleon's disastrous invasion of Russia.

1813.   Prosperity.

Industry flourishes, except for severe cotton strike, Scotland; rapidly rising commodity prices; active speculation; increased foreign trade.

Money easy; large gold premium.

Abundant harvest, sharp fall in farm prices.

Military successes in Spain; coalition of Russia, Prussia, England, and Austria against Napoleon; corn law eased.

Thus climaxed the most rampant price inflation in England until very recent time.*

*The only earlier rival might be the so-called Tudor inflation of the sixteenth century, imprecisely measured because of the dearth of dependable price statistics. In any case, it occurred long before what W. C. Mitchell called a money-making economy in England. Hence the social fabric of the early times would not have felt the impact as it did the inflation of the eighteenth and nineteenth centuries.

1813–1851: DEFLATIONARY; 38 YEARS

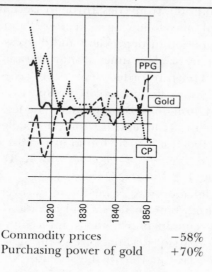

Commodity prices	−58%
Purchasing power of gold	+70%

From the historical peak in 1813 prices fell abruptly and swiftly for 3 years and then continued a generally donward trend for the next 35 years. Agricultural prices already were depressed in 1813, and in the second quarter of 1814 prices in the manufacturing sector followed precipitously, bringing commercial distress and numerous failures. Money tightened and gold went to a record premium.

The year 1815 opened with promise until Napoleon returned from Elba in March. The uncertainty of the Hundred Days had a decidedly dampening effect on the economy. Then came the final defeat at Waterloo in June, touching off a speculative boom that ended in credit collapse and failures by autumn. Commodity prices continued to decline, money tightened, and many country banks failed.

By 1816 England was in a deep depression. There was stagnation of industry and trade generally; the iron and coal industries were paralyzed. In addition, there was a failure of the wheat

crops and below-average harvests in barley and oats. Riots occurred spasmodically from May through December.

These dismal times following soon after Waterloo simply por-
tended a long period of depression and distress, only occasion-
ally punctuated by brighter times of short duration. For 22 of the
next 35 years Thorp recorded depression, recession, and even
panic. Only 9 were designated as prosperity. The industrial
revolution had brought to Britain something less than economic
euphoria. (For the reader who wishes a detailed study of this
period one of the best is to be found in *The Growth and Fluctuation of the British Economy, 1790–1850*, by A. D. Gayer, W. W.
Rostow, and A. J. Schwartz, Oxford, 1953.)

This price deflation was by far the most severe England had
ever experienced, both in depth and duration, granted it also
started at the culmination of an unprecedented price peak.
More than 35 years of declining trend brought prices down to
the level of the last quarter of the seventeenth century.

But for substantially all that period there was one monetary
constant—the price of gold.

As a result the exchange rate between gold and commodities
increased tremendously. On an index basis the purchasing
power of gold increased 70 percent. A man who had gold in his
possession would have had his operational wealth increased by
more than two-thirds. If it was a purpose of the gold standard to
protect the operational wealth represented by gold, it did so very
well. The hard money philosophy propounded by John Locke
150 years before was honored by practice all during this time.

1873–1896: DEFLATIONARY; 23 YEARS

After 1851 prices rose sharply to an index level of 100.0 and
remained on a plateau for two decades; then England plunged
into another major deflation.

Recession hit in the last of 1873 with a stringent money mar-

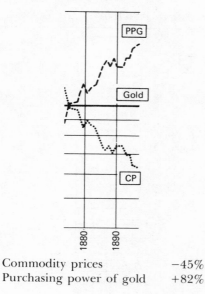

| Commodity prices | −45% |
| Purchasing power of gold | +82% |

ket and very poor wheat harvests. Commodity prices were down before the close of the year, yet exports declined drastically. A long depression was setting in. During the next 23 years Thorp found only 4 that he would label as prosperity; nearly all the rest were years of full depression or recession. Prices reached their low point in the summer of 1896.

Again, the one monetary parameter that held constant was the price of gold at a Mint price of 3 pounds, 17 shillings, 10.5 pence—where Sir Isaac Newton had put it in 1717. The market price was remarkably stable within half a pence of 3 pounds, 17 shillings, 9 pence until the financial panic of 1893, which upped it to 3 pounds, 17 shillings, 10.57 pence for that year.

The operational wealth represented by gold increased enormously. A hoard of gold would exchange for about 80 percent more commodities in 1896 than 20 years earlier.

1897–1920: INFLATIONARY; 23 YEARS

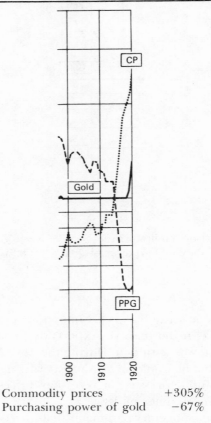

Commodity prices   +305%
Purchasing power of gold   −67%

The year 1897 marked an abrupt change in British price history. Two decades of almost unbroken decline were turned into a rise that culminated 23 years later in a threefold increase. It is true, of course, that a major war intervened. But the rise approximated 40 percent by 1914 and again was more than 30 percent after the Armistice in 1918. From 1914 to 1918 prices went up by 126 percent; and wartime increases are very real for those who suffer them. The point, in any case, is that we are dealing with more here than wartime inflation.

It was a price inflation—and to a large extent was based on surging industrial activity and generally rising economic development. The war years quite aside, Thorp counted 13 years of prosperity and one he characterized as "revival" out of the 19 that remained.

Gold was no match for commodities. Its operational value was cut by two-thirds in an almost continuous decline. By 1920 gold sank to its lowest rate of exchange for commodities in English history.

1920–1933: DEFLATIONARY; 13 YEARS

When American readers hear of the Great Depression they probably think of The Crash of 1929. They may not be aware—or have forgotten—that Europe was suffering during all of the 1920s and suffered its own economic crash in 1920. This was true of France, Germany, Austria, Italy, Sweden, and The Netherlands. It was tragically true of England.

A slump began in summer; employment peaked in April. As early as May a general strike was attempted, and by September employment was in a rapid decline. The financial sector was in a severe depression before the year was out.

Between 1920 and 1933 prices deflated at the highest annual rate in British history for any substantial interval of time. Gold responded sharply with the peaking of commodity prices in early 1920. The index of gold prices had remained constant within one decimal point for 90 years. Then between 1918 and 1920 it increased 33 percent.

Gold was responsive to a commodity price *increase* for the first time in a century. It matched in exact proportion the rise of commodity prices in 1920, and then gold fell away as commodity prices declined, but more slowly than the latter. Once again the *purchasing* power of gold began to rise as a depression phenomenon.

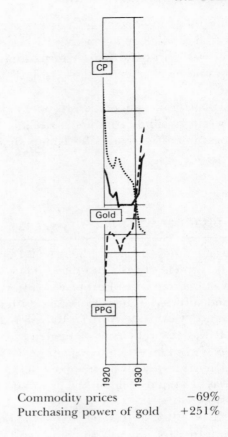

| Commodity prices | −69% |
| Purchasing power of gold | +251% |

1933–1976: INFLATIONARY; 43 YEARS

We have it on the authority of *The Economist* (July 13, 1974) that "Apart from a brief period during the Second World War, when the government rigged the official cost-of-living index with subsidies and controls, prices in Britan have not fallen since 1933." The wholesale commodity price index used here shows the same record, a record which speaks for itself. Superlatives would be superfluous.

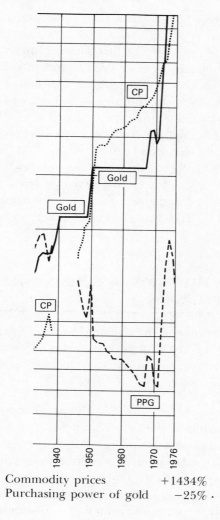

Commodity prices   +1434%
Purchasing power of gold   −25% .

During this time of inflation some of the most interesting operations occurred in the world gold markets in the entire history of commercial and governmental dealings in that metal. These events are discussed on pp. 52–56. For the reader who would look further there is a most understandable account by Timothy Green, *The World of Gold Today*, Arrow Books, London, 1973.

The most striking aspect of this period of price inflation as it relates to gold is that for once gold almost maintained its purchasing power in the face of surging commodity prices.

For a student of gold this period is fascinating. With gold prices free and volatile after the breakup of the London Gold Pool, the metal fought to hold its own versus wholesale commodity prices. In one climactic year it did. In 1974 the purchasing power of gold actually stood 1.5% above its level at the onslaught of inflation in 1933. But in the next two years the persistent inflation triumphed and gold actually fell, so that the purchasing power of gold in 1976 was 25 percent less than in 1933.

A RECAPITULATION OF GOLD IN INFLATION AND DEFLATION

We have now examined the statistical history of price inflation in England over the last four centuries. Let us be certain we are aware of the wide variety of circumstances in which these inflations have taken place.

- Some have occurred in an almost completely agrarian economy, with only the most rudimentary of tools and equipment to aid a productive process largely carried out by human effort alone; others have occurred in predominantly urbanized societies with the highest development of modernization achieved by man. The full scale has been run between labor-intensive and capital-intensive economics, with every degree in between.

- Some have occurred when barter was still a principal means of exchange; some have taken place before the invention of credit currency, when only coins were used as a common denominator for exchange; some have taken place in fully developed money markets, domestic and international, in which the sophistication of finance has reached apogee.

• Some have been associated with wars; some have occurred in moderating peaceful circumstances.

• Some have taken place amidst political turmoil or when the social fabric itself was in danger of being rent; some have had the benign influence of social stability and governmental benevolence.

Out of all these varied circumstances are there some uniform findings about inflation?

First, we must consider how to measure inflation. Several ways have been used for this statistical measurement. These differ by degrees of sophistication and also by the particular view of inflation that the analyst wishes to represent. The following points need to be made:

1. Simplest of all, but perfectly acceptable in some contexts, is the net change in price (or defined price level measurement) from the beginning of the inflationary period to the end. Thus one might say "Inflation has been particularly serious in San Francisco since 1970. The Consumer Price Index has gone up by ——% to 1976." This is a completely meaningful statement, but it represents inflation in its grossest form. That is to say, it reflects both a rate of ascent of prices and the duration of ascent. Within its proper context it is quite acceptable for characterizing the severity of inflation in *that* locality for the time period chosen by the speaker, and it allows for a comparison between two or more localities as long as the time period is the same in the comparisons made.

2. The preceding form of statement breaks down as soon as one wishes to speak of two different periods of inflation of differing duration. It is misleading, if not nonsensical, to make a statement of the following type: "Recent inflation is much more severe in San Francisco than what we had before the

war. Since 1970 the Consumer Price Index went up by ——%
until the start of 1976, but the total increase from 1933 to
1938 was only ——%." The comparison is fallacious because
the *duration* of the period is different in the two cases. Obviously, a way to get around this difficulty is to express inflation
as a *rate* per unit of time.

The simplest way of doing this is to compute the "simple
annual average" rate of inflation (or monthly rate, if you
choose). This takes the net change in prices from beginning
to end and divides by the number of years intervening.
Stated as a rate of change per unit time, it has the clear
advantage of adjusting for the differing lengths of various
periods of inflation, thus allowing for direct comparisons
between their degrees of severity.

3. There is nothing really wrong, or even ambiguous, about the
   form of statistical statement in (2). *It looks back at history.* What
   we often find unsatisfactory about it is that it does not reflect
   the economic sense of inflation as experienced by the *participant.* By its nature, inflation is a compounding process.

   As consumers we feel its surge to a higher level and then,
   as it continues, a surge from that level to a yet higher one.
   Each segment of inflation starts from the higher level already
   created by its predecessors. It is this compounding process
   that the participant experiences. This corresponds mathematically to the phenomenon of compounding interest,
   and we speak of the "average annual compounded
   rate of inflation" and compute our statistical measure accordingly.

For many inflationary periods it makes a distinct difference
which statistical measure we use. For the episodes of English
inflationary history which we have just examined let us present
all so that we may see.

The following observations can be made about the record:

1. The duration of periods of pronounced inflation have been

Years	Duration	Net Change (%)	Simple Average Annual Rate (%)	Average Annual Compounded Inflation Rate (%)
1623–1658	35	+51	+1.5	+1.2
1675–1695	20	+27	+1.4	+1.2
1702–1723	21	+25	+1.2	+1.0
1752–1776	24	+27	+1.1	+1.0
1792–1813	21	+92	+4.4	+3.2
1897–1920	23	+305	+13.3	+6.3
1933–1976	43	+1434	+33.3	+6.6

about the same between the last half of the seventeenth century and the one which we are now experiencing. Two decades plus has been the norm.

2. Although the net changes look impressive, the annual rates of inflation were not at all severe until the twentieth century. This is especially true if we concentrate on the compound rates that commend themselves as more realistic to the statistician. Annual rates of the order of one percent must have been absorbed easily by the participants, even if building up to substantial price increases when continued for more than 20 years.

The inflation associated with the Napoleonic Wars was the first to reach a magnitude noticeable by modern standards. There is no gainsaying its severity. But it is well to remember that it was marked by two highly unusual circumstances: (a) the wars themselves, which were especially embracing and extraordinarily expensive for the thin economies of the times, and (b) the naive financial governance of the Bank of England which was quite unprepared (understandably) to manage for the first time in history a paper-issue currency that was not redeemable in specie.

The other periods of the seventeenth and eighteenth centuries may look imposing on a chart. But we must remember that since they occupied an entire adulthood of that day, their yearly accumulation of inflationary burden was really quite small.

3. This leaves us with the rather surprising conclusion that since the Industrial Revolution, England has experienced only one complete period of inflation from beginning to end—1897 to 1920, *and that the truly severe inflation is a spawn of the Industrial Revolution.*

Economic historians speak of the "English Price Revolution" of the sixteenth century (before this study begins), but R. A. Doughty has recently shown that over the entire major inflationary period commonly so desginated (1519–1629) the average compounded rate was 1.1 percent for industrial products and only about 1.5 percent for agriculture (*Explorations in Economic History 12,* 1975). What is more, the so-called Great Debasement (1540–1560) largely accounted for the increased price quotations of those times.

Let us now look in the same way at the periods designated as deflationary in our price history of England.

Years	Duration	Net Change (%)	Simple Average Annual Rate (%)	Average Annual Compound Rate (%)
1658–1669	11	−21	−1.9	−2.1
1813–1851	38	−58	−1.5	−2.2
1873–1896	23	−45	−2.0	−2.6
1920–1933	13	−69	−5.3	−8.5

- Since 1800 England has had about as many years of deflation as inflation—74 years as compared with 78 (but we must be very much aware of definitions).

- The most recent deflation was by far the most severe. It was sharp and deep as compared with the rest.
- There have been an equal number of periods of deflation and inflation since 1792, that is, since the Industrial Revolution.

Having summarized inflations and deflations separately, we are now in a position to draw together the experience with gold in each of them. From earlier results we have the following net changes in the index of prices and the purchasing power of gold:

	Inflation		Deflation	
	Prices (%)	Purchasing Power of Gold (%)	Prices (%)	Purchasing Power of Gold (%)
1623–1658	+51	−34		
1658–1669			−21	+42
1675–1695	+27	−21		
1702–1723	+25	−22		
1752–1776	+27	−21		
1792–1813	+92	−27		
1813–1851			−58	+70
1873–1896			−45	+82
1897–1920	+305	−67		
1920–1933			−69	+251
1933–1976	+1434	−25		

The evidence drawn from the English experience for 400 years is clear. Gold is no hedge against inflation of a prolonged character. Even worse, it *lost* operational wealth consistently and seriously in each inflationary episode. In the first inflation of modern time, and the only one to have gone its complete course (1897–1920), a person would have lost two-thirds of his operational wealth just by holding gold in bars from beginning to end. And this was in the golden age of the gold standard.

Even more striking, in the current inflationary distress starting with 1933, gold started losing in purchasing power as early
as 1936 and has been deficient by 1933 standards until it just
evened up at the peak of the gold boom in 1974. Already it has
again receded in purchasing power, standing at 25 percent *below*
its 1933 level in 1976. *And this during times when gold prices per
ounce went to their highest prices in history.*

A curious but not contradictory characteristic of gold is that
although it consistently loses purchasing power *within* inflationary periods, it tends to hold its operational wealth reasonably
well from peak to peak of inflation. This is illustrated in the
following set of numbers for which 1930 = 100.0:

Peak Year	Purchasing Power of Gold Index
1658	88
1695	101
1723	98
1776	95
1813	76
1920	79
1976	136

In fact, if one stays out of periods of extended inflation or
deflation, gold does hold to its purchasing power, quite well over
long periods of time. Let us take arbitrarily every fiftieth year
starting with 1600:

Year	Purchasing Power of Gold Index
1600	125
1650	97
1700	120
1750	111
1800	76
1850	111
1900	143
1950	103

Now in a manner similar to that for inflation, let us regard the behavior of the purchasing power of gold in the history of deflations.

Four pronounced price deflations took place in the four centuries recorded, with the three most severe occurring since 1800. In all four price recessions operational wealth in the form of gold appreciated handsomely. When one sees that just by holding gold for 13 years from 1920 to 1933 operational wealth would have increased 2½ times, one realizes that gold can be a valuable hedge in *deflation*, however, poor in inflation.

The historical capability of gold as a hedge against deflation may, however, be contingent on the willingness of government to maintain stable the price of gold.

In the foregoing analyses of inflation and deflation we purposely considered major epochs of each. Consequently, our conclusions necessarily pertained to what happens to the operational wealth of gold with extended inflation—with extended deflation.

PURCHASING POWER OF GOLD IN THE SHORT RUN

Now we might question: How about the short run? Is gold a good way of protecting operational wealth on a year-to-year basis?

The most direct and sensitive way to answer this is to observe the association between price level changes from one year to the next and the concomitant changes in the purchasing power of gold. More directly and technically, we may correlate the first differences between the commodity price index on the one hand, and the index of purchasing power of gold on the other. Chart III shows the results of such a tabulation for the last fully realized inflationary period, 1897–1920.

Year-by-year *changes*, measured in percentage points, of the commodity price index are plotted horizontally. Against these are plotted the corresponding changes in the index of purchas-

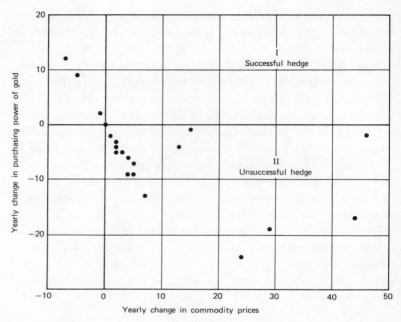

Chart III **Yearly Changes:** Purchasing Power of Gold and Commodity Prices, 1897–1920

ing power of gold. For example, from 1915 to 1916 the commodity price index changed by +29 (i.e., from 111.3 to 140.2). Between the same years the index of purchasing power of gold changed by −18 (i.e., from 89.7 to 71.2). Thus the corresponding point on the correlation chart can be found at +29 on the horizontal scale and at −18 on the vertical axis. In this way the association between changes in the two variables can be plotted for the entire inflationary period on the one chart.

Whenever a plotted point falls somewhere within the second quadrant (lower right-hand sector), it signifies a year for which prices increased and the purchasing power of gold fell. Whenever a point falls in the fourth quadrant (upper left-hand sector), it denotes a year for which prices decreased and purchasing power of gold rose. When a point falls directly at the coördinates (0,0), it represents a case in which neither prices nor gold purchasing power changed. It is only when a change in price took place which was perfectly compensated for by a change in gold that a point would fall on the horizontal line.

In reading the chart we see that 16 points fall in the second quadrant. This means that on 16 occasions the price index jumped and the purchasing power of gold fell. Three points fell in the fourth quadrant. Hence on three occasions the price index decreased and the purchasing power of gold went up. In only one case (i.e., in the first quadrant), was an increase in commodity prices compensated for by an increase in the price of gold—in fact the purchasing power of gold went up in that instance.

The summary measure that characterizes statistically the direction and degree of statistical association is the correlation coefficient. For the data in the correlation chart this value is $r = -.53$.

Rather than reproduce the correlation charts to show graphically how poorly gold served as a hedge against commodity price increase in all the inflations and deflations of English history, only the correlation coefficients for each episode are given.

Inflations

Years	r
1623–1658	−.98
1675–1695	−.99
1702–1723	−.99
1752–1776	−.96
1792–1813	−.85
1897–1920	−.52

We have just seen graphically how poor the hedging ability of gold was for short-run fluctuations in 1897–1920, yet the negative value for r is a moderate figure of −.52. The much higher *negative* values for r in the other inflationary periods suggest that gold hedged even more poorly in them. The curious reader can make up his own correlation charts for those periods using data in Tables 1 and 3. We need not go through the exercise of repeating them here.*

What does deserve further attention is the inflationary period we are still in. This experience cannot be understood unless we distinguish between the time before the two-tier gold market and the period after the two-tier market came into being on March 27, 1968; hence our separate periods should be 1933–1967 and 1968 through 1976.

For the span of inflation from 1933 through 1967 there were 24 increases in commodity prices from one year to the next. On only 4 of these occasions did gold hold its own, either maintaining or increasing purchasing power. Gold failed as a hedge 80 percent of the time. The correlation coefficient was $r = -.62$.

When the two-tier market was performing, starting in 1968 and coming up through 1976, there were 9 successive increases in commodity prices. On 4 of these occasions gold did well, in the sense that it outperformed the commodity markets and showed annual increases in purchasing power.

The overall record for 1933 through 1976 has 33 annual increases in the commodity price index, with 8 occasions when gold held or gained in purchasing power. In this sense gold served as a short-run hedge against price increases less than one-quarter of the time after the turning point in 1933.

A NOTE ON THE RELATION OF COMMODITY PRICES TO GOLD

As we have said, the purchasing power of gold depends on the relation of commodity prices to gold prices. A close scrutiny of this relationship over time discloses an affinity of a curiously

*The reader may be interested in the similar short-run correlation coefficients for the periods of deflation. They are

Years	r
1658–1669	−.76
1813–1851	−.80
1873–1896	−.93
1920–1933	−.88

responsive character. It could be called the "Retrieval Phenomenon," meaning that the commodity price level may move away
higher or lower, but it tends to return repeatedly to the.level of
gold.

Let me explain. By using the same base 1930 = 100.0 for all
index numbers, all three have a common reference level in that
year. This, of course, is a great advantage of index numbers:
statistical time series that originate in terms of quite different
units and orders of magnitude can be made comparable by
computing their values as percentages of a common base period.
In the present instance this means that we can compare directly
in Chart I the line representing the commodity price index and
the line representing the price of gold. When, for example, I
state as a kind of statistical shorthand that commodity prices
equalled gold prices in 1870, the meaning is that their index
numbers were equal in that year relative to their respective
common base of 1930 values equal 100.0. We are thus comparing relative values and not absolutes.

The reader should now scrutinize Chart I and notice how
commodity prices weave around gold prices but always return to
the relationship that held between them in 1930. Let us follow
this process using the shorthand mode of expression described
previously.

As early as 1650 commodity prices had risen to equate with
gold. They passed down through the gold parity level in 1660
and lay below until they rose to touch gold again in 1695 (93.7
and 94.7, respectively).

Again commodity prices dipped below gold, until in 1710
commodity prices moved up to meet the more stable gold price
index. They remained in a constant relation to each other until
1720 when commodity prices fell sharply away from gold, not to
return until 1740.

The next disparity developed shortly after 1745, when commodity prices again fell away from gold price levels, always the
more stable of the two. But by 1765 the retrieval phenomenon
had reasserted itself, and commodity prices rose to meet the
level of gold.

Between 1765 and 1793 commodity prices again fell generally below gold levels but (to put it anthropomorphically) seemed to be striving constantly to reach up for gold, witness 1771, 1776, 1782, and 1790. Commodity prices broke through the gold level in 1793 and stayed above until they fell back down to meet gold in 1815.

After the Napoleonic disturbance, gold resumed its prewar index level in 1820 *and commodity prices fell to join it in 1822.* Thereafter through 1875 commodity prices arced above and below the constant level of gold but always returned to the latter.

After 1875 (when they stood at 99.0 and 99.8, respectively) a divergence developed until 1915, when, characteristically, commodity prices finally moved upward to meet gold. Commodity prices continued to climb past gold until they peaked in 1920. In the decline that followed they homed in again on gold until the two index numbers necessarily were equated in the common base year 1930 = 100.0.

The imagery here is that for nearly three centuries the level of gold was the loadstone for commodity prices. The latter traced a pattern falling and rising around the gold price level but always returning to it before wandering off again.

This long chapter can be summarized with impressive brevity:

SUMMARY

- Gold is a poor hedge against major inflation.
- Gold appreciates in operational wealth in major deflations.
- Gold is an abysmal hedge against yearly commodity price increases.
- Nevertheless, gold maintains its purchasing power over long periods of time, for example, half-century intervals. The amazing aspect of this conclusion is that this is not because gold eventually moves toward commodity prices but because commodity prices return to gold.

PART TWO

THE AMERICAN EXPERIENCE

6 The Evolution of the Gold Standard and Historical Fluctuations in Gold Prices

The English experience has been given major emphasis in this book because of its long duration and the quantity of statistical data which recorded it. The American colonies were, of course, English, and their settlers felt themselves to be Englishmen. Anglo-Saxon law prevailed; cultural attitudes toward money and monetary affairs were similar. One of the shared concepts was the need for, and importance of, a sound currency—and that meant one ultimately based on the precious metals.

The statistical analysis of the American Experience begins with 1800. Well-recognized price data go back to that time. To start any earlier would be dealing with a sparse economy not yet settled down from the rending of ties with Britain.

Wholesale prices are used for the same reasons as with England:

- They are more prevalent, especially for early times, than are retail prices;
- They seem the more rational choice for measuring the purchasing power of gold, because if holders of bullion *were* to buy goods it would more likely be in wholesale markets than at the retail level.

Gold prices are Treasury buying prices throughout most of the period. But when market prices diverged significantly, as during the suspension of specie payments in the Civil War, they are used instead. (W. C. Mitchell, *Gold, Prices, and Wages Under the Greenback Standard,* 1908, Table 1.) Unlike the chapters on England, there is no need in the text for an extended discussion of index number construction, because no *new* index needed to be devised for the American analysis. What have been used on a spliced basis are

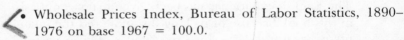

- Wholesale Prices Index, Bureau of Labor Statistics, 1890–1976 on base 1967 = 100.0.
- Wholesale Price Index, Warren and Pearson, 1749–1890 on base 1910–1914 = 100.0.·

Both are given in Appendix B.

All index numbers are on the base 1930 = 100.0. Comparability with the English analysis is not the only reason. This year also represents the termination of a long period of gold price stability in the United States and one of the last years before going off the conventional gold standard and into gold price gyrations of an unusual character.

A BRIEF HISTORY OF THE EVOLUTION OF THE GOLD STANDARD IN THE UNITED STATES

Money was a rarity in early colonial times. The meager stock colonists brought with them was soon expended for imports, and the export of specie from England was forbidden by law. With considerable ingenuity the settlers turned to a sophisticated form of barter.

The English government forbade the production of coins in the colonies. Massachusetts tried as early as 1652, but Charles II ordered the Mint closed because it infringed on the royal prerogative.

Foreign currency (i.e., non-English) early became a substantial medium. Piracy was a considerable source of this, and the slightly more genteel practice of privateering made its contribution. We may not like to acknowledge the rascality of our forebears, but it sometimes had its economic advantages.

Of course, much of the source of this foreign currency was legitimate trade, especially with the Spanish West Indies. Coins were in voluminous circulation in the Spanish possession bordering the Atlantic. Much minting of the silver from the Mexican, Peruvian and Bolivian mines never left the Western Hemisphere, and early trade brought its share to the English colonies. Gold coins from Portuguese Brazil flowed in as well.

A dominant coin of the colonies was the Spanish dollar (a corruption of the germanic "Thaler"). It can be said that the separation of the colonies from England began in the monetary field.

It was in New York that the English monetary policy met with its strongest resistance. Parliament finally felt compelled to permit the New York assembly to issue "paper bills of credit." These were actually treasury notes accorded public receivability. Thus a legitimate paper currency came into being, and other colonies followed suit.

Benjamin Franklin was a great proponent of paper money

and saw in it a way of expanding trade within the colonies while using only a small base of gold.

The prevalence of paper at the time of the creation of the United States, and the expansion of its use thereafter, probably helps to explain why gold coins in this country have never had the deep symbolic significance accorded them in some European countries. The proverbial French peasant and his hoard of buried gold simply did not have an historical counterpart in the colonial freeman.

The monetary affairs of the growing colonies and the fiscal problems of financing the Revolution have been treated thoroughly elsewhere and are not of particular concern in this brief history of the establishment of the gold standard in the United States. Let us, therefore, go on to the first major event in the development of the gold standard.

When President Washington took office he appointed his military aide-de-camp as Secretary of the Treasury. This seeming bit of military nepotism put Alexander Hamilton in charge of our nascent monetary affairs.

One of the greatest achievements of Hamilton was the Coinage Act of April 2, 1792, officially titled, "Act Establishing a Mint and Regulating the Coins of the United States." The Act drew directly from a remarkable document by Hamilton, *Report on the Establishment of a Mint.*

Hamilton considered carefully the merits of a gold versus silver basis for the currency and finally recommended in his *Report* a bimetallic standard. In his own words:

> That the unit, in the coins of the United States, ought to correspond with 24 grains and ¾ of a grain of pure gold, and with 371 grains and ¼ of a grain of pure silver, each answering to a dollar in the money of account.

He also recommended a decimal system of denomination.

A debate ensued in the Congress based on Hamilton's recommendations, but the discussion was largely centered on whether George Washington's portrait should be stamped on the face of a coin rather than an emblem of Liberty.

The Coinage Act of 1792 created a bimetallic system. The two kinds of standard money were linked together and were accorded identical standing under law. This system worked reasonably well until the Civil War, although there was constant haggling in and out of Congress about the proper gold-to-silver ratio (it had been established by the Act of 1792 as 15:1), and some fine tuning periodically was made.

In the cataclysm of the Civil War all banks suspended specie payment by December 30, 1861, and the U.S. Treasury soon followed. The government created legal-tender note issues, and the country went on a paper-money standard on which it remained until January 1, 1879.

While on the paper standard, Congress carried out in 1873 a revision and codification of the Mint and coinage laws. Few silver coins of any denomination were in circulation, and nearly all silver dollars had long before been exported to the Orient in connection with foreign trade or had otherwise disappeared. Consequently, the public was not familiar with the American silver dollar of which they had seen few. Thus when Congress in its codification of 1873 *omitted* the silver dollar in its listing of future coins, no public attention was aroused by the omission. The legal effect, however, was that the right of free coinage of silver at the Mint had been discontinued, and, therefore, legal bimetallism, which had been established by the Mint Act of 1792, no longer existed. When the United States returned to a specie basis on January 1, 1879 it discovered it was de facto on a monometallic gold standard as gold was the only metal accorded the privilege of free coinage in the codification of 1873.

This I would call gold-standard-by-oversight. Some nineteenth-century commentators were not so generous. Epithets such as "frauds," "cheaters," and "liars" were aimed at congressmen. Many silver supporters called it *The Crime of 1873*. A certain segment of Americans has always been emotional about silver (vide the "Cross of Gold" speech by William Jennings

Bryan which gained him the nomination for the Presidency).

The bitter accusations of the press and partisan speakers of the time were not deserved by Congress. Whatever they did, or rather failed to do, was probably not done with the deviousness their critics charged. J. L. Laughlin in his *History of Bimetallism in the United States* (1896) specifically addresses "The charge that silver was demonitized surreptitiously." He found that experts to whom the draft bill was sent for technical comment had pointed out the omission of the silver dollar and its consequences.

But Congress *was* legally liquidating the bimetallic standard when it passed the revision of 1873. And, as Laughlin writes:

> When the bill came before Congress . . . the Senate occupied its time chiefly on questions of seniorage and abrasion, and the House on a question of salaries of officials.

Because the action of 1873 had omitted the silver dollar the Resumption Act, effective January 1, 1879, firmly transferred the United States to gold monometallism. Another world currency had gone on the gold standard.

One cannot miss the irony that two of the great currencies of history, managed by two of the great democracies, both went onto the gold standard quite successfully without public debate of the portentous issues involved, or indeed without a general awareness of what was taking place.*

The gold standard in America was finally formally recognized by the Gold Standard Act of 1900, which provided a definitive legal recognition of what had been in operation since January 1, 1879. With the haste and impetuosity of which Americans are often accused, the United States gave legal recognition in 21

---

*Perhaps this unawareness extended to the Chief Executive Officer. President Grant wrote a personal letter eight months later extolling silver as "the standard value the world over," which was by then true for neither the world nor his own United States.

years to a de facto situation, whereas the more deliberate English had taken a century.

HISTORICAL FLUCTUATIONS IN GOLD PRICES

Chart IV depicts for the entire period 1800 through 1976 the behavior of the price of gold, wholesale commodity prices, and the purchasing power of gold. The relevant data are in Tables 6, 7 and 8, respectively. The last is the rate of exchange between gold and other commodities expressed on a base of 1930= 100.0.

From the time of the Coinage Act of 1792 until March 10, 1933 the United States was on a form of gold standard whether jointly with silver or functioning alone.* The official price of gold was, consequently, established by the various Acts of Congress. Market prices were congruent with those so long as bank notes were redeemable in gold, and this was true except for the suspensión of specie payments between 1861 and 1879.

Since the wisdom of Congress was to keep the price of gold almost constant until the early 1930s, this accounts for the near-rigidity of line of gold price in Chart IV until 1933.

On March 10, 1933 President Roosevelt, relying on the Emergency Banking Act, prohibited by executive order the export of gold and gold certificates *as well as payments in gold by banks*. The United States was, of course, then off the classic gold standard.

At the end of August 1933 the President authorized the Treasury to purchase gold at $29.62 an ounce, which was a move from the pre-existing statutory price of $20.67. On October 25, 1933 the purchase price was raised to $31.36 in a similar manner.

---

*To put a fine point on it, President Wilson did bar the free export of gold between September 1917 and June 1918 using, oddly enough, the Espionage Act of June 1917. The domestic convertibility of notes into gold remained legal, however, and that is probably the key point of the gold standard in the popular conception.

In accord with a presidential message of January 15, 1934 Congress enacted on January 30 the Gold Reserve Act, which gave an entirely new basis to the American monetary system. No more gold was to be coined—all was to be kept in bars. The new gold weight of the dollar was to be as proclaimed by the President alone.

On the next day the President made his proclamation. Although couched in more technical terms, the essence of this decree was that the new price of gold was to be $35.00 per fine ounce. However, since no gold coins were to be issued, and no paper money was to be redeemed in gold, the gold *coin* standard was abandoned. Nor was the gold *bullion* standard adopted under which, up to 1931, the Bank of England had to sell bullion to all comers at a specified minimum of paper money. Yet *a new kind of gold standard* was put in place, since the concept was upheld that the exclusive definition of the monetary unit was to be in terms of gold. But henceforth the gold value of the dollar was to be *managed* by the Treasury.

After 141 years of relative orthodoxy the United States in one year purposely induced a monetary revolution. The graphic results are shown in Chart IV.

Table 6

THE INDEX OF THE PRICE OF GOLD

United States 1800–1976

(1930 = 100.0)

Year	Index	Year	Index	Year	Index
1800	93.8	1831	93.8	1862	113.3
1801	93.8	1832	93.8	1863	145.2
1802	93.8	1833	93.8	1864	203.3
1803	93.8	1834	97.0	1865	157.3
1804	93.8	1835	100.0	1866	140.9
1805	93.8	1836	100.0	1867	138.2
1806	93.8	1837	100.0	1868	139.7
1807	93.8	1838	100.0	1869	133.0
1808	93.8	1839	100.0		
1809	93.8			1870	114.9
		1840	100.0	1871	111.7
1810	93.8	1841	100.0	1872	112.4
1811	93.8	1842	100.0	1873	113.8
1812	93.8	1843	100.0	1874	111.2
1813	93.8	1844	100.0	1875	114.9
1814	93.8	1845	100.0	1876	111.5
1815	93.8	1846	100.0	1877	104.8
1816	93.8	1847	100.0	1878	100.8
1817	93.8	1848	100.0	1879	100.0
1818	93.8	1849	100.0		
1819	93.8			1880	100.0
		1850	100.0	1881	100.0
1820	93.8	1851	100.0	1882	100.0
1821	93.8	1852	100.0	1883	100.0
1822	93.8	1853	100.0	1884	100.0
1823	93.8	1854	100.0	1885	100.0
1824	93.8	1855	100.0	1886	100.0
1825	93.8	1856	100.0	1887	100.0
1826	93.8	1857	100.0	1888	100.0
1827	93.8	1858	100.0	1889	100.0
1828	93.8	1859	100.0		
1829	93.8			1890	100.0
		1860	100.0	1891	100.0
1830	93.8	1861	100.0	1892	100.0

Table 6 (Continued)

Year	Index	Year	Index	Year	Index
1893	100.0	1921	100.0	1950	169.3
1894	100.0	1922	100.0	1951	169.3
1895	100.0	1923	100.0	1952	169.3
1896	100.0	1924	100.0	1953	169.3
1897	100.0	1925	100.0	1954	169.3
1898	100.0	1926	100.0	1955	169.3
1899	100.0	1927	100.0	1956	169.3
		1928	100.0	1957	169.3
1900	100.0	1929	100.0	1958	169.3
1901	100.0			1959	169.3
1902	100.0	1930	100.0		
1903	100.0	1931	100.0		
1904	100.0	1932	100.0	1960	169.3
1905	100.0	1933	100.0	1961	169.3
1906	100.0	1934	169.3	1962	169.3
1907	100.0	1935	169.3	1963	169.3
1908	100.0	1936	169.3	1964	169.3
1909	100.0	1937	169.3	1965	169.3
		1938	169.3	1966	169.3
1910	100.0	1939	169.3	1967	169.3
1911	100.0			1968	190.0
1912	100.0	1940	169.3	1969	200.0
1913	100.0	1941	169.3		
1914	100.0	1942	169.3		
1915	100.0	1943	169.3	1970	176.1
1916	100.0	1944	169.3	1971	199.6
1917	100.0	1945	169.3	1972	283.4
1918	100.0	1946	169.3	1973	473.2
1919	100.0	1947	169.3	1974	772.7
		1948	169.3	1975	781.5
1920	100.0	1949	169.3	1976	612.3

Table 7

THE INDEX OF WHOLESALE COMMODITY PRICES

United States 1800–1976

(1930 = 100.0)

Year	Index	Year	Index	Year	Index
1800	102.2	1831	74.4	1862	82.5
1801	112.6	1832	75.3	1863	105.4
1802	92.8	1833	75.3	1864	153.1
1803	93.5	1834	71.3	1865	146.6
1804	100.0	1835	79.4	1866	137.9
1805	111.9	1836	90.4	1867	128.5
1806	106.3	1837	91.3	1868	125.3
1807	103.1	1838	87.2	1869	119.7
1808	91.3	1839	88.8		
1809	103.1			1870	107.0
		1840	75.3	1871	103.1
1810	103.8	1841	72.9	1872	107.8
1811	100.0	1842	65.0	1873	105.4
1812	103.8	1843	59.4	1874	100.0
1813	128.5	1844	61.0	1875	93.5
1814	144.4	1845	65.9	1876	87.2
1815	134.8	1846	65.9	1877	84.1
1816	119.7	1847	71.3	1878	72.2
1817	119.7	1848	65.0	1879	71.3
1818	116.6	1849	65.0		
1819	99.1			1880	79.4
		1850	66.6	1881	81.6
1820	84.1	1851	65.9	1882	85.7
1821	84.1	1852	69.7	1883	80.0
1822	84.1	1853	76.9	1884	73.8
1823	81.6	1854	85.7	1885	67.5
1824	77.8	1855	87.2	1886	65.0
1825	81.6	1856	83.2	1887	67.5
1826	78.5	1857	88.1	1888	68.2
1827	77.8	1858	73.8	1889	64.1
1828	76.9	1859	76.3		
1829	76.2			1890	65.0
		1860	73.8	1891	64.6
1830	72.2	1861	70.6	1892	60.3

Table 7 (Continued)

Year	Index	Year	Index	Year	Index
1893	61.9	1921	113.0	1950	183.4
1894	55.4	1922	111.9	1951	204.3
1895	56.5	1923	116.4	1952	198.7
1896	53.8	1924	113.5	1953	196.0
1897	53.8	1925	119.7	1954	196.4
1898	56.1	1926	115.7	1955	196.9
1899	60.3	1927	110.5	1956	203.4
		1928	112.1	1957	209.2
1900	64.8	1929	110.1	1958	212.1
1901	63.9			1959	212.6
1902	68.2	1930	100.0		
1903	69.1	1931	84.3		
1904	69.1	1932	75.3	1960	212.6
1905	69.5	1933	76.2	1961	212.1
1906	71.5	1934	86.5	1962	212.6
1907	75.3	1935	92.6	1963	211.9
1908	72.9	1936	93.5	1964	212.3
1909	78.3	1937	99.8	1965	216.6
		1938	90.8	1966	223.8
1910	81.4	1939	89.2	1967	224.2
1911	75.1			1968	229.8
1912	80.0	1940	90.8	1969	238.8
1913	80.7	1941	101.1		
1914	78.7	1942	114.1		
1915	80.5	1943	120.2	1970	247.5
1916	98.9	1944	120.2	1971	255.4
1917	135.9	1945	122.4	1972	267.0
1918	152.0	1946	139.7	1973	302.0
1919	160.3	1947	171.5	1974	359.0
		1948	185.7	1975	392.2
1920	178.7	1949	176.5	1976	410.2

Table 8

THE INDEX OF PURCHASING POWER OF GOLD

United States 1800–1976

(1930 = 100.0)

Year	Index	Year	Index	Year	Index
1800	91.8	1831	126.1	1862	137.3
1801	83.3	1832	124.6	1863	137.8
1802	101.1	1833	124.6	1864	132.8
1803	100.3	1834	136.0	1865	107.3
1804	93.8	1835	125.9	1866	102.2
1805	83.8	1836	110.6	1867	107.5
1806	88.2	1837	109.5	1868	111.5
1807	91.0	1838	114.7	1869	111.1
1808	102.7	1839	112.6		
1809	91.0			1870	107.4
		1840	132.8	1871	108.3
1810	90.4	1841	137.2	1872	104.3
1811	93.8	1842	153.8	1873	108.0
1812	90.4	1843	168.4	1874	111.2
1813	73.0	1844	163.9	1875	122.9
1814	65.0	1845	151.7	1876	127.9
1815	69.6	1846	151.7	1877	124.6
1816	78.4	1847	140.3	1878	139.6
1817	78.4	1848	153.8	1879	140.3
1818	80.4	1849	153.8		
1819	94.7			1880	125.9
		1850	150.2	1881	122.5
1820	111.5	1851	151.7	1882	116.7
1821	115.9	1852	143.5	1883	125.0
1822	111.5	1853	130.0	1884	135.5
1823	115.0	1854	116.7	1885	148.1
1824	120.6	1855	114.7	1886	153.8
1825	115.0	1856	120.2	1887	148.1
1826	119.5	1857	113.5	1888	146.6
1827	120.6	1858	135.5	1889	156.0
1828	122.0	1859	132.8		
1829	123.1			1890	153.8
		1860	135.5	1891	154.8
1830	129.9	1861	141.6	1892	165.8

Table 8 (Continued)

Year	Index	Year	Index	Year	Index
1893	161.6	1921	88.5	1950	92.3
1894	180.5	1922	89.4	1951	82.9
1895	177.0	1923	85.9	1952	85.2
1896	185.9	1924	88.1	1953	86.4
1897	185.9	1925	83.5	1954	86.2
1898	178.3	1926	86.4	1955	86.0
1899	165.8	1927	90.5	1956	83.2
		1928	89.2	1957	80.9
1900	154.3	1929	90.8	1958	79.8
1901	156.5			1959	79.6
1902	146.6	1930	100.0		
1903	144.7	1931	118.6		
1904	144.7	1932	132.8	1960	79.6
1905	143.9	1933	131.2	1961	79.8
1906	139.9	1934	195.7	1962	79.6
1907	132.8	1935	182.8	1963	79.9
1908	137.2	1936	181.1	1964	79.7
1909	127.7	1937	169.6	1965	78.2
		1938	186.5	1966	75.6
1910	122.9	1939	189.8	1967	75.5
1911	133.2			1968	82.7
1912	125.0	1940	186.5	1969	84.1
1913	123.9	1941	167.5		
1914	127.1	1942	148.4		
1915	124.2	1943	140.8	1970	71.2
1916	101.1	1944	140.8	1971	78.2
1917	73.6	1945	138.3	1972	106.1
1918	65.8	1946	121.2	1973	156.7
1919	62.4	1947	98.7	1974	215.2
		1948	91.2	1975	199.3
1920	56.0	1949	5.9	1976	149.3

Chart IV   **The Ameri**
modities, and Purchas

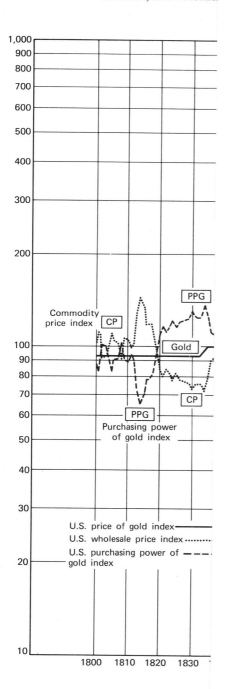

U.S. price of gold index———
U.S. wholesale price index·········
U.S. purchasing power of ———
gold index

7 The Purchasing Power of Gold

Because of the near-rigidity of the price of gold from 1800 to 1933, the curve of the purchasing power of gold is largely a mirror-image of the fluctuations in commodity prices.

Further, as early as 1802, the rate of exchange between commodities and gold was the same as it was to be 128 years later, in 1930. And the wholesale commodity price index, which already stood at 100.0 in 1799, was to show no upward or downward trend all the way to the base year 1930 = 100.0. This will be a startling revelation to those who have thought that the history of prices in the United States was one long upward trend.

There were long swings upward and downward along this steady plane. But the "Retrieval Phenomenon" discovered in the English experience was repeated in this country. Whether ascending for a time, or falling away

149

for substantial intervals, commodity prices turned back toward the steady level of gold prices.

One of the most interesting periods in American history for the gold historian is the "greenback" period—when paper notes were not redeemable in gold. This is the span from 1861 to 1879.

There was an outpouring of inconvertible paper money with only the promise that the government would somehow redeem it someday—a government that might not even survive a civil war. Concurrently, there was a tremendous demand for commodities of all sorts for the military and the civilian populace. Normal sources of production were strained on both counts. The most drastic price inflation the country had ever known occurred in consequence. This was an ideal time to test the hypothesis that gold is a conservator of operational wealth in the face of commodity price inflation.

Let us trace out chronologically and in detail what happened in Chart IV between 1861 and 1879. All numbers are index-based on 1930 = 100.0.

In three years (1862, 1863, 1864) wholesale commodity prices soared by 117 percent—an *annual* rate of +39 percent which has not been matched before or since (1915 to 1920 was at an annual rate of +24 percent).

The price of gold responded with alacrity. By 1864 it had risen to an index of 203.3 for an *annual* rate of +34 percent, but not enough for gold to hold its purchasing power, down by 6.2 percent only—but it was down.

Thereafter, gold's purchasing power continued to decline into the greenback period until it had fallen by −28 percent in 1866. As late as 1872 it was still −24 percent below its level at the initiation of the greenbacks in 1861. Following this poor record gold's rate of exchange for commodities began to improve gradually, until by 1879, when specie payments were resumed, it was just back up to its level when specie payments had been suspended.

Characteristically, gold regained its purchasing power not because it pursued commodity prices successfully, but because commodity prices fell back toward gold—the Retrieval Phenomenon again.

A NOTE ON AN INTERNATIONAL COMPARISON DURING SUSPENSION OF SPECIE

It is instructive to compare the Napoleonic period in England with the Civil War in the United States, *not* because both were military operations, but rather because a similar monetary phenomenon occurred in each. The times were different, but monetary maneuvers were the same. We make a simple time-shift to accommodate the comparison. The date in England is February 26, 1797; the time in America is December 1861.

Up to those points in time the monetary system was strong in both countries and was based on the redemption of paper notes by precious metal. On the dates noted each country negated specie payments. The Bank of England ceased redemption of bank notes by governmental decree. In America the banks had largely ceased to honor their own notes by December 30, 1861, and the U.S. Treasury followed suit early in 1862. Thereafter both countries were on a paper standard for a number of years—England until 1821, and the United States until 1879. That is the crux of the comparison.

Chart V depicts the English and American experience in terms of commodity prices and the attendant behavior of the purchasing power of gold. The completely persuasive feature of this chart is that the purchasing power of gold behaved almost identically in these countries when gold no longer backed the paper currency. This is brought out by comparing the two heavy lines.

Commodity prices immediately inflated in terms of paper currency in both instances. Their inflation continued so long as unredeemable paper money continued, although following somewhat different patterns of rise and decline.

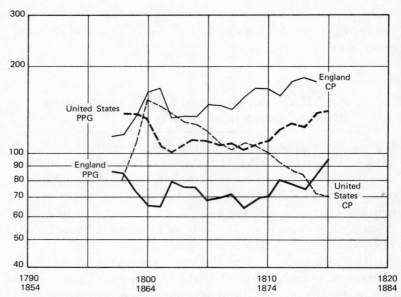

Chart V **Purchasing Power of Gold:** Suspension of Specie, Napoleonic Wars, and the Civil War: 1930 = 100.0

But the two curves of the purchasing power of gold are amazingly alike. In both instances gold lost in operational wealth when conventional wisdom would have expected it to be a haven for purchasing power. And the time-pattern of loss was very much the same in both periods of economic disturbance and political instability. When confidence was lost in the currencies, the purchasing power of gold lost as well.

In both cases gold's purchasing power finally returned to where it had been before the suspension of payments, and it did this by commodity prices returning toward the price of gold.

PURCHASING POWER OF GOLD AFTER SPECIE PAYMENT RESUMED

After the resumption of specie payment for paper currency in 1876 the price of gold stabilized and held at $20.67 through most of 1933. In consequence, fluctuations in the purchasing power of gold again became a mirror reflection of changes in the commodity price level.

At the end of January 1934 the price of gold was set at $35.00 per ounce by Presidential proclamation, an increase of 60 percent. Commodity prices began to rise, but much more slowly, so that the purchasing power of gold increased dramatically, as can be seen in Chart IV. Between 1934 and 1940 gold's purchasing power was on a plane higher than at any time in American history.

But commodity prices began to accelerate rapidly toward the price level of gold following 1939. By 1947 the purchasing power of gold was back to the equivalent of the 1930 level, and the gains in operational wealth were finally erased by the Retrieval Phenomenon operating on the upward side.

From 1947 through 1970 gold's purchasing power sank to lower and lower levels as commodity price inflation outstripped gold prices. Then in the 5 years following 1970 gold streaked upward in a phenomenon unparalleled in American history. Commodity price increases also were striking but no match for the price of gold. The purchasing power of gold increased by 180 percent in those 5 years, and the holders of gold were highly rewarded in operational wealth.

But gold peaked out in 1975 with an annual index number of 781.5, barely higher than the 772.7 for 1974. For 1976 it was down to 612.3. The wholesale price index number continued to rise inexorably.

Is the Retrieval Phenomenon again at work?

In the preceding section we followed the purchasing power of gold chronologically from 1800 through 1976 in the United States. Inflationary and deflationary periods were encountered, with some intervals of price stability falling between. All these periods were treated in time order as they developed a linear history of the operational wealth represented by gold.

Now let us go back and collect the separate episodes of price inflation to find if there are any generalities we can discover for these, and in a similar way to gather for collective analysis all the periods of price deflation. Certain economic and historical events that occurred during these episodes are included.

This is the schema we used in Chapter 5 for England. In that chapter there is a discussion of the difficulties of definition lurking in the terms "inflation" and "deflation." Here, I will simply point out that the terms are used solely as descriptive of price behavior.

With all the caveats I expressed earlier I would select the following episodes of price history for the United States:

Inflationary	Deflationary
1808–1814	1814–1830
1843–1857	
1861–1864	1864–1897
1897–1920	1929–1933
1933–1951	
1951–1976	

1808–1814: INFLATIONARY; 6 YEARS

The first period of sustained price inflation, after the establishment of the United States as an independently governed economy, began to be felt in 1809, although it had its antecedents in the preceding years. War with England was already threatening in 1807 when trade restrictions became severe. By 1808 the paralysis along the coast had spread inland. Complete stagnation set in for the industrial centers of New England by 1809, and in agriculture an abnormally small wheat crop sent that price sharply upward. The United States was supported by an extremely thin economy at that time and was hyperreactive to shocks of these kinds. The inflation was shortage induced. The closure of the United States Bank in 1811 further weakened confidence in the youthful economy.

Commodity prices	+58%
Purchasing power of gold	−37%

Great Britain declared war in June 1812 and laid an absolute blockade along the coast. In 1813 and 1814 prices continued to soar, and there was no surcease until peace was declared in December of the latter year. Wholesale commodity prices had gone up nearly 60 percent in 6 years. The purchasing power of gold declined by almost 40 percent.

1814–1830: DEFLATIONARY; 16 YEARS

Imports flooded the United States in the first quarter of 1815. Speculation in new land had been growing in the past few years, and now there were many failures. Money became very tight in financial centers, and the failures of speculation added to the financial chaos. The military victory at New Orleans was ironic since it came after our surrender to the British and during the most severe economic disarray of the new nation.

Unemployment in 1816 was severe and aggravated by the

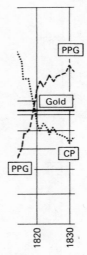

| Commodity prices | −50% |
| Purchasing power of gold | +100% |

enormous imports flooding the domestic markets. The second United States Bank was organized by the middle of the year but afforded no help; credit contractions caused widespread financial difficulties by 1818. It shocks our sensibilities in an account of economic history to recall that some humans were marketed, but it must be noted that the collapse of speculation in the slave markets of the South added to the economic difficulties of the nation.

Incidentally, the availability of vast public lands in the new nation was not the unmitigated blessing we might suppose. There was much speculative purchasing of land. Shortages of credit led to forced selling that contributed to the confusion.

Dullness in trade and industry continued. Trade decreased further when in 1826 England forbade her remaining colonies to deal with the United States. The election of Jackson to the Presidency in 1828 did not help the business climate, and his message of hostility to the United States Bank in December 1830 simply confirmed the fears of the business and financial community.

The holders of gold did very well during this period. Their operational wealth doubled just by standing pat.

1843–1857: INFLATIONARY; 14 YEARS

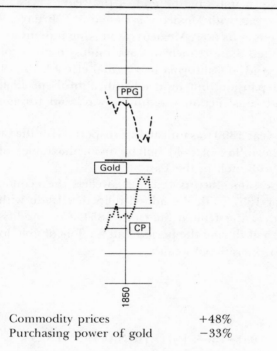

Commodity prices	+48%
Purchasing power of gold	−33%

No dramatic events marked the onset of this inflationary period. Prosperity gradually swelled and became general again by 1845. Active railroad speculation began, and wheat speculation was rife by the last quarter.

In 1846 war with Mexico was declared in May. The Oregon controversy with England was settled in June. Foreign trade was completely revitalized and thriving in 1847. Great domestic activity in trade and industry brought about full employment.

There were swift victories in Mexico, with the capture of Vera Cruz in March and Mexico City, itself, in September. The United States was an ebullient, chauvinistic nation by now.

Gold was discovered in California in January 1848, and what can be called a California boom gave a great psychological lift to the Eastern states by the end of the year.

The treaty with Mexico was signed in February. Strange as it may seem to us now, Mexico was making indemnity payment to the United States which was a stimulus to our economy.

The gold in California had a dual effect by 1849. It encouraged expansion, but induced unhealthful speculations. Active railroad construction was under way, and foreign trade was booming.

The year 1850 was unusually prosperous for the same reasons. And the influx of gold bullion from the mines of California began to be felt in the East.

These same factors fed and swelled the economy through most of 1857, with the added fillip that trade with Japan was opened to the United States in 1854. Commodity prices rose almost half during the period, but holders of gold lost one-third of their operational wealth.

1861–1864: INFLATIONARY; 3 YEARS

This, of course, was the period of our War Between the States. From the monetary standpoint the main event was the suspension of specie payment and the unsupported flood of greenbacks. This phenomenon has been discussed at length elsewhere.

Commodity prices soared and gold took off overnight. The average price of the latter doubled by 1864, but commodity prices went up even faster. Gold almost held its purchasing

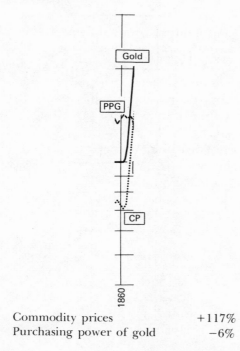

| Commodity prices | +117% |
| Purchasing power of gold | −6% |

power but lost in operational wealth by −6 percent, obviously doing far better than greenbacks, which were a national disaster.

1864–1897: DEFLATIONARY; 33 YEARS

The postwar depression was tragic and prolonged, although it had its bright spots between 1880 and 1885.

Lee surrendered in April of 1865. Lincoln was assassinated in the same month. The Civil War was formally ended in August. The South was in economic chaos, with a complete collapse of currency and government finance.

As early as 1866 there was a slackening of trade in the North. The economic record for years thereafter until 1879 (the year of resumption of specie payment) is a dreary account.

Commodity prices	−65%
Purchasing power of gold	+40%

The years 1880 through 1885 were comparatively good, but even in 1884 there were numerous bank failures, and the device of issuing clearing house certificates for money was employed.

Labor strife became severe. The Anti-Chinese riots of 1885 were symptomatic. In 1886 the Knights of Labor went on railroad strike, widespread coal strikes were called, and the "Haymarket Massacre" exploded in Chicago.

Matters wobbled along until 1893, when extreme depression was felt in the last half of the year. Business failures were prevalent, and a new type hit the country: railroads went into receiverships.

The year 1894 was one of deep depression as well. Serious strikes occurred in the bituminous coal industry, railroads again were struck, and Coxey's armies marched in the spring of the year. Intense depression was suffered in 1896, and commodity prices hit a bottom in 1897.

Operational wealth would have increased by 40 percent if gold had been held for this extended period and the temptation to liquidate had been resisted.

1897–1920: INFLATIONARY; 23 YEARS

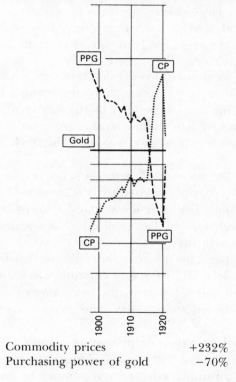

| Commodity prices | +232% |
| Purchasing power of gold | −70% |

It was in the 1890s that business cycles began to take on an international pattern.

In the United States prosperity returned in 1898. The era of industrial combinations began. The short war with Spain started in April and ended in August. The Philippines and the Hawaiian Islands were acquired. The boom in immigration began in 1899, carrying all the implications that were to follow for the supply of labor and the demands for industrial output.

The years 1900 and 1901 were ones of great prosperity. Many records for production were established. The achievement of economies of large-scale industry was epitomized by the U.S. Steel Corporation, formed in the latter year.

There were numerous labor troubles in 1903, but immigration was very large. By 1905 great expansion was taking place with iron and steel in the vanguard. A new phenomenon of prosperity was seen in the land: severe railroad freight congestion was endemic.

Prosperity continued throughout 1906 and until the autumn of 1907. Then panic struck and the financial sector was paralyzed. This was touched off by the failure of the Knickerbocker Trust Company; many banks suspended payments, and clearing house certificates were issued. The stock exchange collapsed.

The year 1908 was one of depression, but revival set in during 1909. Real prosperity returned for 1912 and 1913. In the latter year the Income Tax Amendment to the Constitution was ratified, but surely no one then realized what a business force this was to become in the economy of the twentieth century.

Curiously, perhaps, the first year of World War I was a time of depression in the United States; certainly foreign trade fell off drastically. By 1915, however, the beginning of war industries manufacturing led to recovery, and exports increased enormously.

The record of economic prosperity continued through the war and until the last half of 1920. Then industrial orders were cancelled at an unprecedented rate, money became extremely tight, and there was a near collapse in the stock and bond markets. Prohibition became effective in January, and Harding was elected in November.

In the period 1897–1920 the operational wealth of gold fell by 70 percent.

1929–1933: DEFLATIONARY; 4 YEARS

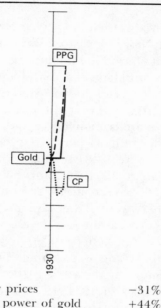

Commodity prices	−31%
Purchasing power of gold	+44%

The United States saw a tremendous drop in prices in the single year from 1920 to 1921 (−37%), but thereafter, unlike England, wholesale commodity prices held steady until 1929. As a deflationary period, therefore, we count from 1929 on.

The Great Depression did not catch American economists by surprise to the same extent it did the general public. Warning signals were evident before. Agriculture had been in recession during most of the 1920s, without any signs of recovery. Economists were well aware of the tendencies of business cycles to become international, and Europe was already in a state of depression. The signals were there, which is not to say they were widely heeded.

The spectacular behavior of the stock market disguised the fact that the American economy was moving toward complete disarray. Public attention was focused instead on the booming activity of the stock exchanges to an extent unprecedented in American history.

The first shock was felt in October, 1929 with the collapse of prices on the New York Stock Exchange. There followed a certain amount of soothing public utterances about mere paper values and the fundamental soundness of America. But the domestic economy, running poorly and with growing unemployment since the end of 1929, was in serious trouble.

Bank failures are economic tragedies in themselves, but they are also an index of more pervasive problems. At the beginning of 1930 there were 24,079 banks; 1352 of these suspended payments in 1930. In 1931 bank failures rose to 2294. An additional 1456 expired in 1932. From January until March 1933 alone, there were 408 new failures.

Banking disasters at the local level are the kinds of economic events everyone can understand. The national psychology was reversed abruptly. The overconfidence of the late 1920s turned to deep pessimism by the early 1930s.

In the latter part of 1931 the second shock was felt. It was foreign in origin and fundamental, because it struck at the monetary base of our economy. European countries—Austria, Germany, then England and France—were no longer able to meet their debts. Their exportation of gold was placed under "exchange controls." The various gold standards were abandoned, and national currencies were disarranged. Around $2 billion of American investments abroad suddenly became next to worthless.

The rapid decrease in the amount of commercial paper eligible for the issuance of Federal Reserve notes increasingly meant that the notes had to be backed by gold. The demand for currency was increasing enormously because of the public's growing distrust of banks. The Glass-Steagall Act was hurriedly passed in February 1932 authorizing the Federal Reserve Banks to use government bonds for 1 year instead of commercial paper as collateral for Federal Reserve notes. Even this might not have assuaged the public if the 40-percent gold reserve had not been maintained.

But confidence in the solvency of banks continued to fade. Some writers have inferred from this a comparable lack of confidence in the national currency. This was not true. People in large volume withdrew their deposits from banks to *secure currency*. It is undoubtedly true that some of the latter was then converted into gold, but certainly not in the same measure. (This period has been very well covered by Milton Friedman and Anna Schwartz in their *Monetary History of the United States, 1897–1960*.)

That portion of the American public which was sufficiently alarmed to create an internal drain on gold was joined by foreign creditors and investors. During February 1933, and until Roosevelt's inauguration on March 4, $624 million in gold was withdrawn from the Treasury and the Federal Reserve Banks.

On Monday, March 6, at one o'clock in the morning the newly sworn in President Roosevelt declared the nationwide bank holiday. After the bank holiday an uneasy calm prevailed. On Monday, March 13, 4507 national banks and 567 state member banks were allowed to open for normal business. This was more than three-quarters of the member banks of the Federal Reserve System.

After these reopenings, public confidence in banking was restored. Bank withdrawals were redeposited to a large extent, and gold was returned to exchange for the more convenient paper money.

On March 12, 1933 President Roosevelt had given the first of his "fireside chats," his most influential and important speech until the attack on Pearl Harbor.

The precipitous decline in wholesale prices had ended by the close of 1933. Gold was a very good way to have held wealth from 1929 until that time, not as a protection against *inflation*—

because quite the opposite was happening—but because operational wealth was thereby enhanced.

The people had rushed to gold not to protect themselves from price inflation, but because of what I call the "Attila Effect" in Chapter 8.

This period, 1929–1933, ended with the United States in deep trouble. Commodity prices had fallen by 31 percent in 4 years, but it should be noted that the operational wealth of gold had gone up by nearly 45 percent.

1933–1951: INFLATIONARY; 18 YEARS

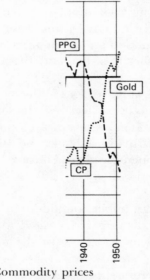

Commodity prices   +168%
Purchasing power of gold   −37%

On January 30, 1934 Congress passed the Gold Reserve Act which overturned the American monetary system. The coinage of gold was discontinued. All gold was to be kept in bars as the property of the United States government through one or another of its agencies. The gold content of the dollar could be redefined by proclamation of the President, which meant, of course, that he could change the price of gold by edict.

The next day Roosevelt issued his proclamation fixing the "weight of the gold dollar" at 15 5/21 grains, 9/10 fine. Since there was no such thing as a "gold dollar," the effect was to fix the standard unit of value known as a dollar at 15 5/21 grains of gold 9/10 fine. The choice of 15 5/21 grains is explained by the fact that 9/10 of this, namely 13 5/7 grains of gold fine, multiplied by 35, represented the market price of an ounce of fine gold. The actual price of gold was accordingly reset at $35 = 1 ounce. The depreciation amounted to 40.94 percent.

No gold coin was to be produced at the new level, and no paper money was to be redeemed in gold; the gold *coin* standard was abandoned, the gold *bullion* standard was not used to replace it. Yet a *kind* of gold standard was upheld: the monetary unit called the "dollar" was exclusively defined in terms of gold.

The short-run purpose for which Roosevelt seems to have undertaken this long-run move, and how he failed of that purpose, are vividly discussed by John Kenneth Galbraith in *Money*, Chapters XIV and XV. All that needs to be noted here is that the immediate stimulus to commodity prices which Roosevelt sought did not come about. And the long upward move from 1933 to 1951 was due to a host of other factors, including the outbreak of World War II in 1939.

The United States gold price stood at $35 per ounce from 1934 through 1951, that is, the entire period under present discussion. The high point of the purchasing power of gold in all United States history to that date occurred in 1934 through the action of President Roosevelt, as just described. Thereafter, slowly, and with some backtracking, commodity prices began to rise.

Gold's purchasing power held up rather well until 1940, when commodity prices began a steady rise to 1951. Because of this rise the purchasing power of gold suffered continuous erosion. Just between 1940 and 1951 it fell off by 56%.

Gold would have been a dismal holding for a United States citizen as a wartime haven for his wealth, even had personal possession been legally possible.

1951–1976: INFLATIONARY; 25 YEARS

| Commodity prices | +101% |
| Purchasing power of gold | +80% |

Part 1. *1951–1970: Inflationary; 19 years*

| Commodity prices | +21% |
| Purchasing power of gold | −14% |

Part 2. *1970–1976:*

| Commodity prices | +66% |
| Purchasing power of gold | +110% |

The criterion of inflation in this book is rapidly rising prices.
Based solely on that criterion the period from 1951 through

1975 is one continuous episode. And the major heading and corresponding figures listed first above represent that entire episode from beginning to end.

In this case, however, it is important to focus separately on the subperiod of the first 19 years, from 1951 through 1970, and on the last 6, because of the unprecedented sprint in gold prices following 1970.

Until 1970 the pattern observed in England for four centuries, and always in America since 1800, continued to hold: commodity prices went up and the purchasing power of gold went down.

But from 1970 through 1975 a new phenomenon occurred; wholesale commodity prices went up by 58%, yet the purchasing power of gold shot up with *an increase of 180%*. A unique reversal had taken place with the momentous leap in gold prices in those 5 years. Why did it happen?

The stage was set for this event by the dissolution of the London Gold Pool in 1968 and the emergence of the two-tier market in that year. Thereafter, monetary gold would be used for official settlements only within a closed system of central banks, the United States agreeing to sell to other nations from its own gold reserve at $35 per ounce. The other tier was for private buyers who could purchase legally on open markets at prices set by supply and demand (see Chapter 2).

A RECAPITULATION OF GOLD IN INFLATION AND DEFLATION IN THE UNITED STATES

In 1800 the United States were 16 in number and largely concentrated along the Atlantic coast. With the admission of California in 1850 the United States had established itself firmly on the other side of a vast land mass. For decades thereafter, the demographic and economic history of the nation was dominated by the opportunities for growth between the two oceans.

Throughout this period and up to the present, we have reviewed the price history of the country and focused on episodes of inflation and deflation. Let us now draw these two kinds of episodes together and see if any generalizations can be made with regard to them, respectively, and especially to examine the behavior of the purchasing power of gold in each.

First we summarize with regard to inflation. Several ways are used for the statistical measurement of the extent of inflation. These differ by degrees of sophistication and by the particular view of inflation that the statistician wishes to represent. In order of complexity there are these three:

1. The net change in price, or some defined price level measurement, from the beginning to the end of a designated inflationary period;
2. The simple annual average rate of inflation obtained by dividing the net change in (1.) by the number of years involved, in the case of annual data;
3. The average compounded inflation rate. (For a fuller discussion of these measures and their merits see pp. 121–2, Chapter 5.)

A statistical summary of the inflationary episodes in the United States since 1800 is as follows:

Years	Duration	Net Change (%)	Simple Average Annual Rate (%)	Average Annual Compound Rate (%)
1808–1814	6	+ 58	+ 9.7	+ 7.9
1843–1857	14	+ 48	+ 3.4	+ 2.8
1861–1864	3	+117	+39.0	+29.5
1897–1920	23	+232	+10.1	+ 5.4
1933–1951	18	+168	+ 9.3	+ 5.6
1951–1976	25	+101	+ 4.0	+ 2.8

Let us now look in a similar way at periods of deflation in the United States:

Years	Duration	Net Change (%)	Simple Average Annual Rate (%)	Average Annual Compound Rate (%)
1814–1830	16	−50	−3.1	−4.2
1864–1897	33	−65	−2.0	−3.1
1929–1933	4	−31	−7.8	−8.9

We observe:

- Since 1800 the United States has had many more years of inflation than deflation (88 years versus 58).
- There have been twice as many periods of inflation as deflation (but we must be aware of definition).
- The most recent deflation was short, sharp, and at an annual rate most severe of all.

Now that we have summarized periods of inflation and deflation separately for the United States we are in a position to draw together the experience with gold in each of them. From earlier results we have the following net changes in the index of wholesale prices and the purchasing power of gold.

The evidence drawn from the American experience is convincing even though not completely consistent. In five out of the six major inflationary periods of American history since the eighteenth century, gold has lost its purchasing power. And quite severely so in four of those five.

The one exception to the loss of purchasing power appears from 1951 through 1976. As was pointed out earlier even this exceptional period followed the typical pattern of loss in gold's purchasing power until 1970, with commodity prices up 21

| | Inflation | | Deflation | |
Years	Prices (%)	Purchasing Power of Gold (%)	Prices (%)	Purchasing Power of Gold (%)
1808–1814	+58	−37		
1814–1830			−50	+100
1843–1857	+48	−33		
1861–1864	+117	−6		
1864–1897			−65	+40
1897–1920	+232	−70		
1929–1933			−31	+44
1933–1951	+168	−37		
1951–1976	+101	+80		

percent from 1951 and gold's power to buy (operational wealth) down 14 percent.

To repeat, the evidence is convincing even if a deviation is found among the inflationary years of 1970–1975: when inflation sets in, the purchasing power of gold declines.

No exceptions are found for periods of deflation: in all three since 1800 operational wealth represented by gold has appreciated handsomely.

In the long view gold has held its purchasing power very well in the United States. As early as 1802 it exchanged for wholesale commodities at the same rate it did in 1930. This commodity-equivalence, relative to the base year 1930 = 100.0, also was realized in such disparate years as listed on p. 173.

Thus we observe purchasing power of gold moving along a horizontal plane for 170 years of American history. We have yet to see if this long-run constancy has been fundamentally disturbed by recent events, or whether the experience of 1970–1976 is only an aberration. Will the Retrieval Phenomenon again become operative?

Year	Purchasing Power of Gold
1802	101.1
1820	111.5
1836	110.6
1855	114.7
1865	107.3
1874	111.2
1882	116.7
1916	101.1
1927	90.5
1947	98.7
1972	106.1

PURCHASING POWER OF GOLD IN THE SHORT RUN

In the foregoing analyses of inflation and deflation we have purposely considered extended episodes of each. In consequence, our conclusions necessarily pertained to the operational wealth of gold in major price inflations and deflations.

Now we might question: how about the short run? Does gold hold its purchasing power on a year-by-year basis?

The most direct and sensitive way to answer these questions is to observe the statistical association between price level changes from one year to the next and the concomitant changes in the purchasing power of gold. More directly and technically, we will correlate the first differences of the commodity price index on the one hand with the first differences of the index of the purchasing power of gold on the other.

One way to formulate the model is as follows:

1. If the purchasing power of gold holds steady, all first differences in the annual index are zero.

2. If commodity prices fluctuate, all first differences in the annual index are not zero.

3. Therefore, if the purchasing power of gold is constant, the coefficient of correlation between (1) and (2) is necessarily zero.

The advantage of this model is that it allows one to test directly the null hypothesis that $r = 0.0$ by established procedures.

If $r \gtrless 0.0$ by a statistically significant amount, gold is not a perfect hedge against price changes. Further, the closer r is to a limit of -1.0, the poorer is the hedge.

The correlation coefficients for the separate periods of inflation and deflation appear as follows:

Inflation

Years	r
1808–1814	−.96
1843–1857	−.97
1861–1864	−.37
1897–1920	−.82
1933–1951	−.54
1951–1975	+.70

Deflation

1814–1830	−.92
1864–1897	−.42
1929–1933	−.96

All but one are significant at the 10 percent level and most reach the 5 percent level of significance as well. The one exception is the value $r = -0.37$ for the Civil War years. Only three first differences constitute the sample in this case, and the null hypothesis cannot be rejected.

In all other instances the evidence is compelling that gold is indeed a poor hedge against annual price fluctuations.

SUMMARY

The conclusions to be drawn from the American experience are very much like those based on the English analysis.

- Gold is a poor hedge against major inflations.
- Gold appreciates in operational wealth in major deflations.
- Gold is an ineffective hedge against yearly commodity price increases.
- Nevertheless, gold does maintain its purchasing power over long periods of time. The intriguing aspect of this conclusion is that it is not because gold eventually moves toward commodity prices but because commodity prices return to gold.

8 Reflections on the Golden Constant

The purpose of this book is to create an objective, analytical study of the monetary history of gold and its purchasing power in England and the United States over as long a span of time as trustworthy records are available. While engaged in the necessary reading, thinking, and writing I tried to winnow out any bias or feelings of partisanship from whatever source, and to present only those facts, and conclusions based on facts, supportable by evidence.

In the course of assimilating so much material over so long a time, various ideas, hypotheses, and impressions formed in my mind—not susceptible to test at that time, or even addressable by the customary methods of science, but nevertheless of possible interest and use to the reader. This chapter contains a series of such thoughts, gathered together under the loose term "reflections."

THE ATTILA EFFECT

It is not easy to be dispassionate where gold is concerned. However scientific one may try to be, there is a nagging feeling that something deeper than conscious thought, not an instinct but perhaps a race-memory, distorts perspective. For gold is inexorably entwined with two of man's primordial needs: the imperative to survive and the desire to possess and enjoy beauty.

We know that primitive man found shining pebbles in a stream and carried them carefully to his shelter. The nuggets shone like the sun he worshipped, they were responsive to his touch, and were easily worked into adornments that never corroded and were coveted by others.

In time he learned that those pebbles could be exchanged for food or shelter or warmth. Possession of them meant security for himself and those he sought to protect.

As the centuries passed, his trust in the metal was reinforced again and again. When the Four Horsemen galloped, a stock of gold pieces, cunningly concealed or surreptitiously carried, has often meant the difference between living and dying. Thus gold became synonymous with security and safety in folk wisdom. I have no doubt that such feelings still prevail.

Historically, gold has served as a financial refuge in political, economic, and personal catastrophes. This I call the Attila Effect and examples are legion. To cite a few:

- The Latifundia passed gold bars secretly to their heirs who thus survived barbarian invasions to become nobility under the Merovingian kings of the fourth century.
- White Russians who escaped the Bolsheviks survived on treasures they carried in flight.
- Austrian refugees, escaping Hitler's storm troopers, often owed their survival in a new country to the gold and jewels they could carry on their persons.

The French peasant was astute when he buried his coins on the threat of invasion and pillage. Anyone who fears the collapse of his country's currency is acting rationally when he shelters his assets in gold. It is when these judicious measures are translated into a strategy for protection against recurring price inflations that the reasoning breaks down. This is the lesson my statistics have taught me.

GOLD AS A HEDGE AGAINTS INFLATION

Andre Sharon, head of the international research department at Drexel Burnham, Inc., notes, "the value of gold essentially derives from its capacity to preserve real capital and purchasing power."* I select this particular quotation because of the prestige of the organization and the position of the spokesman, but statements in this vein can be found in great numbers. They can be traced back for generations and in many countries.

How can this proposition so contrary to statistical fact become so widely believed and quoted? Possibly because gold has preserved capital in cataclysmic cases it is easy to infer that it can be trusted to do the same in less severe circumstances. To extrapolate from gold's protection in singular catastrophes to its use as a strategy against cyclical inflation is an example of faulty inductive reasoning.

THE RETRIEVAL PHENOMENON

The reason why gold is not a satisfactory hedge against inflation (but does very well in periods of deflation) is that gold does not match commodity prices in their cyclical swings. The record of the centuries, as shown on Chart I, is very clear and is broken only by recent events.

Yet over the long run (i.e., periods longer than the price cycles just noted), gold maintains its purchasing power remarkably

*Christian Science Monitor Service, January 11, 1976.

well. Basically this is due to the Retrieval Phenomenon. Gold prices do not chase after commodities; commodity prices return to the index level of gold over and over. This is one of the principal findings of my study.

As a statistician I am in no position to account for this event (when all three index numbers approximate numerical equality), but I do have a feeling for probability. My feeling is that it is beyond rational belief that this event could occur by chance alone, with the observed frequency, over the last three centuries.

On this subject the temptation is particularly intense for me to shed the self-imposed restriction of the Introduction (to speak only as a statistician) and to assay the role of a monetary economist. Were I to explore the latter subject I would begin to surmise as follows: If it is a settled national policy that the price of gold will be held constant, then there will be times when, for various reasons, commodity prices will fall below or rise above that constant level. When either of these swings becomes severe enough, monetary authorities will intervene and adjust the monetary supply to reverse the process. This will tend to return the commodity price level toward the constant price of gold. Not primarily because it is *gold*, but rather because it is *constant*.

But this assumes a fairly sophisticated appreciation of monetary economics on the part of the authorities and the power to exercise their authority. The first appearance of the Retrieval Phenomenon is about 1650, and it shows itself repeatedly in the eighteenth century. The detailed testimony before the Bullion Committee (p. 46) is painfully indicative that the monetary authorities of those days had neither the perspicacity nor the sense of obligation to manage the level of commodity prices.

Furthermore, as Lance E. Davis has written in his commentary on Anna J. Schwartz's paper entitled "Secular Price Change in Historical Perspective,"

Even if we all agree that the stock of money has been an important determinant of the price level, there should be room for other factors in our writing of price history.*

*Journal of Money, Credit and Banking, February 1973, pp. 243–273.

THE GOLD NOSTALGIA

There are those today who feel that a return to "the gold standard" would prove a panacea for all our monetary ills. These arguments surface in public discussions, the press, some best-sellers, and even in parliaments. The impression left is that the gold standard is a mechanism which if left without interference would arrange, in an evenhanded way, the monetary affairs of a nation or even the world.

Recently, the financial editor of a major radio station said, "One of the reasons that gold gives stability is that it is in limited supply and is not vulnerable to printing press politics of governments which inflate and debase their paper currency." Several years ago the Director of the Bank of France declaimed, "Whatever the views of the United States, other nations want to maintain the discipline that only a gold based system can imply, and that paper money cannot guarantee."

My first question to these gentlemen would be, "To what type of gold standard should we return, since history and theory have provided us with several forms?" Of these there are two major ones, the *gold-coin* standard and the *gold-bullion* standard. The first is of paramount significance because it was used in England from 1717 to 1925 and in the United States until Roosevelt's proclamation in March 1933. There is also a third form, of some theoretical interest and occasional instances of actual application, known as the *gold-exchange* standard.

The essential characteristics of the classical gold-coin standard are as follows:

- All forms of money, paper and otherwise, are held at a parity with a coined monetary unit defined by its gold content and are convertible into this gold coin on demand.

- This monetary unit is coined freely, without an appreciable charge for the process itself.

- Gold coins circulate freely and may be freely exported, imported, or melted down.

- Gold is unlimited legal tender.
- Gold constitutes a large part of the nation's central monetary reserve.

The *gold-bullion* standard may have all these features except that special conditions of convertibility are imposed: a stipulated minimum of bullion must be purchased with paper money for the act of redemption to take place. Parliament in the Gold Standard Act of 1925 obligated the Bank of England to sell gold only in bars with a minimum weight of approximately 400 troy ounces at the historic price of 3 pounds, 17 shillings, 10.5 pence. (The same act also removed some other provisions of the classic gold-coin standard.)

Since there are different types of gold standards, some conscious choice must be made to begin with. This implies varying degrees of managing the monetary system at the outset. (For a more extensive discussion see Milton Friedman, "Real and Pseudo Gold Standards," in his *Dollars and Deficits,* pp. 247–265.)

Further along there are at least four pressure points at which a government may have to interfere, whichever form of gold standard is adopted. With some risk of oversimplification, they are as follows:

1. Paper currency does not have a 100 percent gold reserve behind it. There is not enough bullion in the world today to support worldwide trade, commerce, and finance on a one-to-one basis of paper to gold. A fractional reserve is a necessity. Only a government has sufficient authority to set the percentage of gold backing for a circulating paper issue. If a government fixes the reserve at, say, 40 percent, it can by that same authority change it to 20 percent, 15 percent, or whatever it wishes, with attendant inflation of the paper currency. The very act of setting a reserve is a governmental manipulation.

2. The world price of gold may increase (drastically, as it has in the 1970s) so that either the *admissible* volume of paper

currency will automatically inflate or the required reserve ratio of gold will have to be reduced correspondingly.

3. If the price of gold is to be held constant by the marketplace, gold must be bought or sold by the government in quantities precisely decided by the government, or interest rates adjusted by central banks to accomplish the same purpose by indirection.

4. If the price of gold is to be held constant by edict, the market for gold must be interdicted by the government, for example, exports forbidden, imports embargoed, private hoardings outlawed, and so on.

Governmental interference at any one of these points is, of course, a denial of laissez-faire. This is not to say that a gold standard would be impossible today. It *is* to say that the gold standard as a dehumanized, self-disciplining dispenser of monetary justice is a myth.

Any monetary system needs to be managed. The real questions are how and to what extent.

MORE NOSTALGIA

There exists a romanticized nostalgia about the gold standard that leads people to say, "things weren't like this when our money was tied to gold."

This is demonstrably erroneous. There were both serious unemployments and pronounced inflations in England and the United States when the classic gold standard prevailed. Some of the worst records of depression occurred in Great Britain when the gold-coin standard was operative.*

The mysticism that seems to emanate from gold even permeates officialdom at times. Dr. Miller, a member of the Federal

---

*See, for example, Keynes, "The Depression of the Eighteen-Nineties," *A Treatise on Money*, p. 164 ff.

Reserve Board, testified before the United States Committee of Congress on Stabilization in 1927:

> The gold standard means more than a legal undertaking to redeem the currency and credit of a nation in gold. The gold standard, to my mind, means a device which acts as a kind of regulating and levelling influence, so as to keep the price level, credit conditions, and the currency situation in all countries that are of the group that have the gold standard in some sort of proper alignment to one another. To me, the gold standard means a set of practices, a system of procedure, never formulated, never consciously thought out, not invented by anybody, but the growth of experience of the great commercial countries of the world, rather than merely the employment of gold to redeem all forms of obligations.*

This lyrical laissez-faire never did hold, and would not now.

THE LEVEL OF PRICES IN THE VERY LONG RUN

People living today believe that prices for common articles were cheaper in their parents' day and far cheaper for their grandparents. This happens to be true. If we look at the years between 1880 and 1910 for both England and the United States, 30 years of depressed prices can be seen. That accounts for the grandparents. Prices were very low in the 1930s. That accounts for the parents.

However, I suspect that people today then extrapolate backwards into past centuries and conclude that prices have been on an upward trend forever. This is far wide of the mark as shown in my statistical study, especially as illustrated in Chart I. To cite a specific case, the price of four pounds of wheaten bread was a shade higher in London in 1767–1768 than it was in 1934.†

Perhaps the impression we gain that things must have been

*Report of Commissioners, p. 693.
†Mitchell and Deane, *Abstract of British Historical Statistics,* p. 498.

cheaper in the old days comes from the history of wages. Rough calculations made from the *Abstract of British Historical Statistics* and the *Annual Abstract of Statistics* of the Central Statistical Office, London, show that money wage rates of manual workers increased by 4600 percent between 1700 and 1972 in London.

Since the prices of goods were not rising by anything approaching the historic soar of wage rates, the reader might be interested in the rise in "real wages" during almost three centuries. By rough approximation from the two sources just cited, I make this out to be an increase of 695 percent. *An ounce of gold just about held its purchasing power over these centuries, but the value of an hour's labor increased seven-fold.*

Some of the phenomena in price history offer optical illusions, even when we are looking at hard data. For example, consider the first inflationary period noted in this study, 1623 to 1658. This appears in Chart I as a striking rise in prices when we view the line on the chart, and they did go up by more than 50 percent. But this was over a period of 35 years, a lifetime in those days, and the annual compound rate of increase was only 1.2 percent—modest indeed.

For years historians have spoken of the "price revolution" of the sixteenth century. This looks imposing on a graph when we see it all at once. But even at its worst, from 1540 to 1560, the compound rate was 3.6 percent. We would feel fortunate today to have such a moderate rate of price increase.

WHAT IS THE FUTURE?

What of the future of gold? Specifically, are there judgments we can make about its price, since that is one of the themes of this book?

The price of gold when it is the monetary standard is quite a different matter than when it is vulnerable to the forces of a free market. This has been convincingly demonstrated by the two-tier market since 1968.

We cannot form our prediction of gold prices by simple deduction from its price history under the gold standard. In spite of nostalgia, romanticism, and (in some quarters) wishful thinking, the major trading nations will not return to the gold standard, whether coin or bullion.

Without arguing the merits of the case, I foresee a further moving of gold out of the monetary systems of the world. The more this takes place, the greater is the flexibility to be expected in the gold markets.

I look for an increasingly unfettered market for gold. But this is not to say a market self-corrective through the usual demand/supply model, whereby an increase in price will induce an increase in supply, and a fall in price will diminish offerings on the market.

The demand and supply functions for gold are much more complicated than that.

DEMAND

Overlaying the fabrication demand for gold, including adornment, is a strong speculative component especially sensitive to inflation or the prospect thereof. Gold as a commodity for fabrication will rise by inflation along with other metals. If it goes up 5 percent for this reason, it may go up another 5 percent, say, as speculators rush to buy before further inflation hits. A rise in gold prices may not dampen demand, it may actually stimulate demand—such is the popular reputation of gold as a hedge against inflation.

In the language of economics gold has a high elasticity of expectations, that is, the ratio of expected price increases to present price increase is high. In this circumstance the speculative motive tends to feed on itself.

A further unsettling aspect is that the demand for gold is not only a function of inflation but is sensitive to *changes* in the *rate* of inflation. Thus gold fell from $197.50 per ounce in December

1974 to $103.50 in the summer of 1976—not because inflation had ceased, but because the *rate* of increase had fallen. It has at this writing (September 1977) risen to $150, largely because the rate of inflation has again increased *and* the anticipation that the rate of inflation will increase further.

Compounding the complexity of the demand function for gold is that a sudden decrease in its price tends to have a multiplier effect downward. Speculators rush to liquidate their stocks, accelerating the fall in price they are trying to avoid.

SUPPLY

The conventional, self-corrective demand/supply model also is inappropriate for gold because of some peculiarities on the supply side. The market supply of gold comes from two principal sources: mine production and above-surface stocks.

Mine Production

Over the years 1970–1975 about 77 percent of total free-world production came from the mines of South Africa. Obviously, the policy decisions of these companies are of utmost importance in determining the response of gold supply to a change in world prices. South African policy is to mine *ore* of the lowest grade profitable at the prevailing gold price. With ore mining capacity subject to severe physical limitations, the quantity of *gold* produced therefore falls as the gold price rises (see Fells and Glynn, *Gold 1976*, Consolidated Gold Fields Limited, London, 1976). This leads to what the economist calls a "backward-rising" supply curve. It is indeed a rare phenomenon in commodity markets.

The practical effect of this policy was to *reduce* the production of gold from South African mines in every year from 1970 through 1975, whereas the average price received was *rising* from $36 in 1970 to $154 in 1975.

Over the same period, annual gold production from the rest of Africa held about constant. It increased for Latin America and Oceania, fell moderately for Asia, and fell progressively for the United States and Canada.

The net effect was a 25 percent *decrease* in the mined supply of gold in the free world during the 5 years when gold prices rose by an amount unprecedented in history.

This production policy and the phenomenon of the "backward-rising" supply curve is not confined to South Africa. The president of Homestake Mining Company, operator of the largest gold mine in the Western Hemisphere, said in an interview published by the Pacific Coast Coin Exchange in 1974:

> Well, we always try to work as near as we can to our hoist and mill capacity—about 6,600 tons of ore per day. With higher gold prices, it's become profitable for us to mine lower grade ore. So while the amount of ore we process remains about the same, actual gold output is lower. For instance, during 1972, our gold output declined 20 percent from 1971. Yet our income and profits are considerably greater than a few years ago. The situation is similar for gold mines in South Africa.
>
> Over the years, I expect gold production will continue to drop— the faster the price of gold rises, the faster the drop. If gold were at $300 per ounce, I think gold production would be something like a half or third what it is now.

Further to flavor the uncertainty of the price-quantity relation is the 10 percent of free-world gold production that comes as a by-product of base metal mining. This is far more dependent on the factors affecting the markets for the base metals, that is, lead, copper, and so on, than on the price of gold, taken by itself.

Above-Surface Stocks

The offerings from these are by their nature more volatile than mining production. In general they are of two forms: stocks held by central banks and the International Monetary Fund; stocks held by private investors and speculators.

Sales from the first defy analysis in terms of going market price. They are conducted for quite different reasons. Indeed, they are more likely to be price-affective rather than price-reactive (note the auctions of the IMF and sales, rumored or actual, by the United States Treasury).

Hoarding and dishoarding from private stocks is bound to be influenced by available price in the market, but it is difficult to generalize the connection. Probably all that can be said in a general way has been implied by the preceding remarks on the speculative demand component.

Thus it is easy to predict a more nearly free market for gold in the future, with the attendant possibility that gold will become a better hedge against inflation than it has proven over past centuries. But it is quite a different matter to predict the course of gold prices themselves in the short term.

A last source of uncertainty is Russian. We do not know the size of her gold stocks, only that they must be very large. In itself this would not be fatal to prediction; what is an enigma is what Russia will choose to do with her gold.* If we could assume that Russia would be motivated solely on grounds of economic logic (settling her balance of payments, etc.), forecasts would not be particularly hazardous. The truly unsettling prospect is that she might at any time make major moves out of noneconomic venturism and affect the world price of gold in quite unpredictable ways.

THE GOLDEN CONSTANT

As far back as anthropologists have studied cultural organizations, gold has appeared as a constant for the appreciation of

---

*Sometimes playfully, but usefully, called the "Muraviev Margin" after Nikhail Nikolaevich Muraviev, Foreign Minister to Czar Nicholas II, who put Russia on the gold standard in 1899.

beauty, the storage of riches, or the exchange of goods or services.

Gold has two interesting properties: it is cherished and it is indestructible. It is never cast away and it never diminishes, except by outright loss. It can be melted down, but it never changes its chemistry or weight in the process. The ring worn today may contain particles mined in the time of the Pharaohs. In this sense it is also a constant.

In this book we discover the stability of gold in yet another context. Its price has been remarkably similar for centuries at a time. Its purchasing power in the middle of the twentieth century was very nearly the same as in the midst of the seventeenth century.

Thus the title of this volume. But, in spite of the methodology of the analysis, there is no intent to define "constant" in the scientific sense of a mathematical parameter. The concept is at once too universal and too elusive for that. As with gold itself, the title may mean different things to different people.

Appendix A

PROMINENT PRICE INDEX NUMBERS FOR ENGLAND

Prices 1. Indices of British Commodity Prices 1790–1850, Based on the Gayer, Rostow and Schwartz Monthly Indices

NOTES

[1] SOURCE: Annual average of the monthly figures in A. D. Gayer, W. W. Rostow and A. J. Schwartz, *The Growth and Fluctuation of the British Economy 1790–1850* (2 vols., Oxford, 1953), vol. I, pp. 468–70.

[2] The composition and weighting of the indices is as follows:

Domestic		Imported			
Wheat	745	Sugar	166	Pepper	3
Oats	497	Cotton	163	Beeswax	2
Mutton	461	Wool	119	Brimstone	2
Beef	239	Tea	111	Cochineal	2
Coal	216	Raw Silk	61	Isinglass	2
Tallow	132	Tobacco	58	Liquorice	2
Butter	116	Timber	38	Logwood	2
Pork	116	Rum	28	Madder	2
Iron Bars	83	Flax	27	Mahogany	2
Iron Pigs	66	Brandy	22	Shumac	2
Leather Butts	41	Port Wine	22	Annatto	1
Hard Soap	41	Staves	20	Balsam	1

Item	Qty	Item	Qty	Item	Qty
Hides	38	Indigo	19	Barwood	1
Tinplates	21	Hemp	18	Brazilwood	1
Tin	6	Hides	18	Cinnamon	1
Mottled Soap	4	Coffee	18	Cocoa	1
Starch	3	Thrown Silk	13	Fustic	1
Alum	1	Linseed	11	Geneva Spirits	1
Camphor	1	Olive Oil	5	Ginger	1
Linseed Oil	1	Pearl Ashes	4	Jalap	1
Rape Oil	1	Bristles	4	Castor Oil	1
Vitriol	1	Tar	4	Opium	1
Sal-ammoniac	1	Turpentine	4	Whale Oil	1
Clover Seeds	1	Saltpetre	4	Whale Fins	1
		Barilla	3	Quicksilver	1
		Iron	3	Quinine	1

Prices 1. Indices of British Commodity Prices 1790–1850 (cont.)

(Monthly average of 1821-5 = 100)

	Domestic and Imported Commodities	Domestic Commodities	Imported Commodities		Domestic and Imported Commodities	Domestic Commodities	Imported Commodities
1790	89.3	87.1	87.5	1821	99.7	98.4	101.8
1791	89.7	84.5	94.6	1822	87.9	83.9	100.2
1792	88.1	80.6	99.0	1823	97.6	97.0	99.3
1793	96.6	91.6	100.6	1824	101.9	104.2	95.3
1794	98.5	96.3	95.9	1825	113.0	116.5	103.4
1795	114.9	113.6	109.5	1826	100.0	106.7	83.1
1796	116.1	115.8	108.6	1827	99.3	106.2	82.1
1797	106.2	100.8	114.2	1828	96.4	102.9	80.0
1798	107.9	100.2	123.4	1829	95.8	102.8	78.2
1799	124.6	119.9	129.8	1830	94.5	101.7	76.5
1800	151.0	156.6	122.5	1831	95.3	103.0	76.3
1801	155.7	161.7	127.3	1832	91.5	97.9	75.2
1802	122.2	122.3	113.2	1833	88.6	92.2	79.1
1803	123.6	120.4	125.9	1834	86.5	88.4	85.2
1804	124.3	119.7	132.8	1835	84.5	84.3	85.2
1805	136.2	133.5	138.6	1836	95.2	98.4	87.1
1806	134.5	131.9	137.5	1837	94.3	101.6	76.1

Year			
1807	131.2	128.3	137.0
1808	144.5	141.3	152.1
1809	155.0	153.8	157.1
1810	153.4	153.4	151.4
1811	145.4	149.2	133.4
1812	163.7	172.2	141.1
1813	168.9	173.1	155.8
1814	153.7	148.5	167.0
1815	129.9	124.6	144.3
1816	118.6	115.0	128.3
1817	131.9	131.8	130.7
1818	138.7	139.8	133.9
1819	128.1	130.4	120.3
1820	115.4	117.4	108.7

Year			
1838	97.8	106.0	78.0
1839	104.3	113.4	82.2
1840	102.5	110.4	83.1
1841	97.7	105.9	77.9
1842	88.8	95.3	72.5
1843	79.7	84.5	67.6
1844	81.1	86.7	67.2
1845	83.3	92.0	62.9
1846	86.0	97.2	60.8
1847	96.8	114.0	61.3
1848	81.8	94.8	54.1
1849	73.9	81.4	56.1
1850	73.5	77.4	63.3

Prices 2. The Sauerbeck-*Statist* Prices Indices—1846–1938

NOTES

[1] SOURCE: A. Sauerbeck, 'Prices of Commodities and the Precious Metals,' in the *J.S.S.* (1886), continued annually thereafter in the same source by Sauerbeck and subsequently by the editor of *The Statist.*

[2] These indices are based on wholesale prices and unit values of imports.

(Average of 1867–77 = 100)

	Food				Raw Materials				Overall Index
	Vegetable (a)	Animal (b)	Sugar, Tea and Coffee (c)	Total	Minerals (d)	Textile Fibres (e)	Sundry (f)	Total	
1846	106	81	98	95	92	77	86	85	89
1847	129	88	87	105	94	78	86	86	95
1848	92	83	69	84	78	64	77	73	78
1849	79	71	77	76	77	67	75	73	74
1850	74	67	87	75	77	78	80	78	77
1851	73	68	84	74	75	75	79	76	75
1852	80	69	75	75	80	78	84	81	78
1853	100	82	87	91	105	87	101	97	95
1854	120	87	85	101	115	88	109	104	102
1855	120	87	89	101	109	84	109	101	101
1856	109	88	97	99	110	89	109	102	101
1857	105	89	119	102	108	92	119	107	105
1858	87	83	97	88	96	84	102	94	91

Year									
1859	85	85	102	89	98	88	107	98	94
1860	99	91	107	98	97	90	111	100	99
1861	102	91	96	97	91	92	109	99	98
1862	98	86	98	94	91	123	106	107	101
1863	87	85	99	89	93	149	101	115	103
1864	79	89	106	88	96	162	98	119	105
1865	84	97	97	91	91	134	97	108	101
1866	95	96	94	95	91	130	99	107	102
1867	115	89	94	101	87	110	100	100	100
1868	113	88	96	100	85	106	102	99	99
1869	91	96	98	94	89	109	100	100	98
1870	88	98	95	93	89	106	99	99	96
1871	94	100	100	98	93	103	105	101	100
1872	101	101	104	102	127	114	108	115	109
1873	106	109	106	107	141	103	106	114	111
1874	105	103	105	104	116	92	96	100	102
1875	93	108	100	100	101	88	92	93	96
1876	92	108	98	99	90	85	95	91	95
1877	100	101	103	101	84	85	94	89	94
1878	95	101	90	96	74	78	88	81	87
1879	87	94	87	90	73	74	85	78	83
1880	89	101	88	94	79	81	89	84	88
1881	84	101	84	91	77	77	86	80	85
1882	84	104	76	89	79	73	85	80	84

Prices 2. The Sauerbeck-*Statist* Prices Indices—1846–1938 (cont.)
(Average of 1867–77 = 100)

	Food				Raw Materials				Overall Index
	Vegetable (a)	Animal (b)	Sugar, Tea and Coffee (c)	Total	Minerals (d)	Textile Fibres (e)	Sundry (f)	Total	
1883	82	103	77	89	76	70	84	77	82
1884	71	97	63	79	68	68	81	73	76
1885	68	88	63	74	66	65	76	70	72
1886	65	87	60	72	67	63	69	67	69
1887	64	79	67	70	69	65	67	67	68
1888	67	82	65	72	78	64	67	69	70
1889	65	86	75	75	75	70	68	70	72
1890	65	82	70	73	80	66	69	71	72
1891	75	81	71	77	76	59	69	68	72
1892	65	84	69	73	71	57	67	65	68
1893	59	85	75	72	68	59	68	65	68
1894	55	80	65	66	64	53	64	60	63
1895	54	78	62	64	62	52	65	60	62
1896	53	73	59	62	63	54	63	60	61
1897	60	79	52	65	66	51	62	59	62
1898	67	77	51	68	70	51	63	61	64
1899	60	79	53	65	92	58	65	70	68
1900	62	85	54	69	108	66	71	80	75

1901	62	85	46	67	89	60	71	72	70
1902	63	87	41	67	82	61	71	71	69
1903	62	84	44	66	82	66	69	72	69
1904	63	83	50	68	81	71	67	72	70
1905	63	87	52	69	87	72	68	75	72
1906	62	89	46	69	101	80	74	83	77
1907	69	88	48	72	107	77	78	86	80
1908	70	89	48	72	89	62	73	74	73
1909	71	89	50	73	86	64	76	75	74
1910	65	96	54	74	89	73	81	81	78
1911	70	90	61	75	93	76	81	83	80
1912	78	96	62	81	110	76	82	88	85
1913	69	99	54	77	111	84	83	91	85
1914	75	100	58	81	99	81	87	88	85
1915	108	126	70	107	126	92	109	108	108
1916	133	152	86	130	158	129	136	140	136
1917	177	192	113	169	172	192	174	179	179
1918	168	207	130	174	192	222	202	206	192
1919	179	213	147	185	220	228	219	222	206
1920	227	263	198	234	295	262	244	264	251
1921	143	218	83	158	181	140	145	153	155
1922	107	184	82	130	142	134	124	132	131
1923	98	162	101	122	155	140	117	134	129
1924	119	158	105	130	158	170	120	146	139
1925	118	162	89	128	154	165	119	143	136

197

Prices 2. The Sauerbeck-*Statist* Prices Indices—1846–1938 (cont.)

(Average of 1867–77 = 100)

	Food				Raw Materials				Overall Index
	Vegetable (a)	Animal (b)	Sugar, Tea and Coffee (c)	Total	Minerals (d)	Textile Fibres (e)	Sundry (f)	Total	
1926	108	150	88	119	154	133	114	131	126
1927	108	138	83	114	141	131	118	129	122
1928	107	142	78	114	123	136	117	124	120
1929	99	146	72	110	126	122	111	119	115
1930	77	142	54	96	112	84	97	97	97
1931	68	119	50	83	100	63	85	82	83
1932	72	105	50	79	99	64	81	81	80
1933	60	106	47	74	107	67	80	83	79
1934	63	108	50	77	109	72	80	85	82
1935	66	107	42	76	112	80	83	90	84
1936	76	109	41	81	118	83	88	94	89
1937	93	117	49	93	142	93	101	110	102
1938	81	111	43	84	136	75	87	96	91

(a) Viz. English wheat, American wheat, flour, barley, oats, maize, potatoes, and rice.

(b) Viz. prime beef, middling beef, prime mutton, middling mutton, pork, bacon, and butter.

(c) Viz. West Indian sugar, beet sugar, Java sugar, and averages of various types of coffee and tea.

(d) Viz. iron, copper, tin, lead, coal in London, and coal for export.

(e) Viz. uplands cotton, Dhollerah cotton, flax, hemp, jute, English wool, merino wool, and silk.

(f) Viz. hides, leather, tallow, palm oil, olive oil, linseed oil, and seeds, petroleum, soda crystals, nitrate of soda, indigo, and timber.

Prices 3. Board of Trade Wholesale Price Indices—1871–1938

NOTES TO PART A

[1] Source: 18th *Abstract of Labour Statistics* (collected from the *Board of Trade Journal* and revised).
[2] These indices are based on market prices and on unit values of imports and exports.

A. 1871–1920. 1900 = 100

	Coal and Metals (a)	Textile Fibres (b)	Food and Drink					Miscellaneous Materials (g)	Total Index
			Corn, Etc. (c)	Animal Products (d)	Sugar, Tea, Tobacco, etc. (e)	Wine and Foreign Spirits (f)	Total		
1871	68.3	146.4	163.5	110.6	239.2	122.7	144.1	145.1	135.6
1872	102.9	166.5	169.2	111.9	242.1	122.8	147.3	151.5	145.2
1873	128.3	161.9	178.3	119.3	229.7	124.4	153.4	156.8	151.9
1874	104.8	151.1	178.5	120.1	216.2	119.2	152.5	154.5	146.9
1875	84.6	147.3	161.6	127.3	213.4	116.1	148.9	140.3	140.4
1876	72.4	137.9	160.2	127.7	207.9	112.4	148.0	141.1	137.1
1877	67.5	135.2	175.5	125.3	228.2	113.2	154.8	139.3	140.4
1878	62.8	131.4	159.7	121.1	202.6	114.8	144.1	125.1	131.1
1879	58.7	123.0	157.4	114.4	192.0	116.9	138.9	113.8	125.0
1880	64.8	130.0	159.0	116.1	197.1	119.1	140.9	124.4	129.0
1881	61.9	127.6	154.1	116.3	192.9	112.9	138.6	123.0	126.6
1882	62.2	123.4	153.7	122.1	191.3	109.4	141.0	123.7	127.7
1883	60.7	119.1	150.5	123.4	183.6	111.3	139.7	121.6	125.9
1884	57.5	115.2	130.1	114.4	150.4	109.5	123.9	114.5	114.1
1885	54.6	108.9	123.6	104.7	137.6	109.8	115.4	111.4	107.0
1886	52.6	99.9	116.4	100.7	128.9	112.8	109.9	101.7	101.0
1887	53.9	102.7	115.4	96.2	120.8	111.3	106.5	95.3	98.8
1888	56.6	101.2	115.3	102.4	131.4	114.4	110.5	98.0	101.8
1889	62.7	105.1	114.0	101.2	141.2	116.3	110.4	103.1	103.4
1890	74.9	105.4	115.3	99.5	125.3	113.2	108.5	99.4	103.3

199

Prices 3. Board of Trade Wholesale Price Indices—1871–1938 (cont.)

A. 1871–1920. 1900 = 100

	Coal and Metals(a)	Textile Fibres(b)	Food and Drink					Miscellaneous Materials (g)	Total Index
			Corn, etc.(c)	Animal Products (d)	Sugar, Tea, Tobacco, etc.(e)	Wine and Foreign Spirits(f)	Total		
1891	70.1	101.4	134.3	99.7	127.2	113.4	116.3	95.0	106.9
1892	65.2	95.6	117.9	99.9	127.8	110.3	109.9	92.5	101.1
1893	59.0	96.4	108.9	103.6	132.8	112.4	108.6	89.3	99.4
1894	60.0	88.6	100.7	99.4	117.8	109.6	101.9	84.5	93.5
1895	56.8	84.3	100.1	96.0	106.7	108.0	98.9	84.9	90.7
1896	55.5	92.9	92.7	90.1	107.8	112.3	93.3	86.5	88.2
1897	56.3	86.8	101.7	92.5	100.8	116.4	97.4	86.9	90.1
1898	61.7	80.0	117.5	89.8	99.9	113.4	102.2	89.7	93.2
1899	72.4	82.9	101.6	94.5	99.6	103.5	98.0	91.3	92.2
1900	100.0	100.0	100.0	100.0	100.0	100.0	100.0	100.0	100.0
1901	82.2	93.3	102.6	99.3	94.7	96.7	100.1	96.3	96.7
1902	76.1	92.3	102.3	104.4	84.4	91.8	101.4	92.5	96.4
1903	74.1	101.7	102.2	102.1	86.4	99.5	100.6	91.7	96.9
1904	70.9	112.9	106.9	98.3	92.5	100.8	101.2	88.3	98.2
1905	71.3	106.7	104.2	97.7	104.8	107.9	101.2	91.1	97.6
1906	78.3	121.1	102.3	102.2	88.7	103.2	101.0	95.6	100.8
1907	86.9	127.4	109.3	104.8	94.2	100.0	105.5	99.7	106.0
1908	78.5	109.8	113.8	103.3	99.0	97.8	107.0	94.8	103.0
1909	73.6	112.4	114.7	105.8	100.4	99.0	108.7	96.5	104.1
1910	76.6	136.2	105.9	111.7	111.7	100.2	109.2	104.3	108.8
1911	74.7	128.9	114.3	109.2	114.1	104.1	111.6	105.5	109.4
1912	84.9	119.6	124.0	116.8	120.4	111.9	119.9	110.1	114.9
1913	92.5	135.0	118.6	119.6	106.8	106.4	117.7	109.4	116.5
1914	86.7	128.8	118.2	122.7	127.0	102.1	120.9	111.3	117.2
1915	116.7	119.8	163.8	145.9	169.8	87.8	154.1	143.8	143.9

1916	165.8	180.1	209.5	175.1	196.7	103.6	189.4	204.0	186.5
1917	182.0	270.4	272.5	228.8	248.6	136.7	246.2	256.3	243.0
1918	204.9	354.4	259.3	263.8	256.9	210.6	260.3	268.6	268.1
1919	280.2	373.3	287.5	273.7	284.4	244.3	279.7	317.8	296.5
1920	419.2	503.7	354.8	306.8	401.6	265.8	334.1	336.6	368.8

(a) Viz. coal (34), pig iron (15), copper (5), lead (1½), tin (1½), and zinc (1½).

(b) Viz. cotton (38), British wool (6), foreign wool (13), silk (9), flax (4), and jute (3).

(c) Viz. British wheat (14), imported wheat (33), British barley (12), imported barley (5), British oats (17), imported oats (4), maize (8), hops (4), rice (1), and potatoes (33).

(d) Viz. English beef (52), English mutton (31), imported bacon and ham (21), milk (29), butter and margarine (12), imported cheese (4), imported eggs (5), and fish (7).

(e) Viz. sugar (2), tobacco (2), tea (8), coffee (1), and cocoa (1½).

(f) Viz. wine (5), and foreign spirits (1½).

(g) Viz. cotton seed (5), linseed (5), olive oil (1), palm oil (½), paraffin and paraffin wax (½), petroleum (2), rubber (1½), bricks (3), wood and timber (20), and hides (8).

Prices 3. Board of Trade Wholesale Price Indices—1871–1938 (cont.)

NOTES TO PART B

[1] SOURCE: *Board of Trade Journal.*

[2] Statistics separating coal from other minerals, and wool from other textiles, were not published for the year 1920. Combined indices for 1920 and 1921 were as follows:

	Coal and Other Minerals	Wool and Other Textiles
1920	251.5	358.9
1921	178.9	171.6

[3] These indices are based on market prices.

B. 1920–34. 1913 = 100

	Food				Metals and Minerals			Textile Materials			Other Articles	Total Index
	Cereals (a)	Meat and Fish (b)	Other Foods (c)	Total	Coal	Iron and Steel	Other (d)	Cotton	Wool	Other (e)	(f)	(g)
1920	273.4	262.5	278.9	271.8	...	357.8	...	480.2	...	...	272.9	307.3
1921	194.3	218.5	214.1	209.0	242.9	209.9	131.9	192.3	158.3	193.7	195.6	197.2
1922	151.1	172.1	172.3	165.2	171.7	136.8	116.2	182.2	160.6	173.3	166.0	158.8
1923	139.2	155.7	168.4	154.5	179.3	147.2	114.1	201.9	179.2	159.7	161.9	158.9
1924	160.1	153.6	184.4	166.3	172.4	142.9	120.3	227.8	219.0	165.6	157.6	166.2
1925	163.5	161.7	173.2	166.5	146.0	126.0	121.6	209.8	196.9	171.9	157.4	159.1
1926	150.2	153.8	159.7	154.8	184.6	123.5	120.1	158.3	169.5	147.5	145.0	148.1
1927	152.7	137.5	165.4	152.0	133.6	119.9	111.9	154.7	170.2	138.5	142.5	141.6
1928	149.1	140.9	166.7	152.3	117.9	112.3	107.1	164.2	185.9	137.8	142.3	140.3
1929	137.8	146.2	151.9	145.3	124.5	114.2	116.0	154.4	165.6	131.6	135.5	136.5
1930	109.1	140.2	132.4	126.6	121.4	112.7	95.0	121.2	122.4	101.7	123.8	119.5
1931	89.8	116.0	131.0	111.5	123.1	104.9	78.2	96.8	99.9	80.5	105.6	104.2
1932	96.7	105.7	130.4	110.6	123.3	103.7	80.5	95.8	90.2	79.2	96.2	101.6
1933	90.4	107.1	113.3	103.4	122.3	105.8	84.0	96.2	99.9	74.0	101.4	100.9
1934	93.8	110.1	111.2	104.8	126.0	109.6	81.2	106.9	114.2	69.2	105.2	104.1

(a) Viz. wheat (7), barley (5), oats (2), maize (1), and rice (2).

(b) Viz. beef and veal (6), mutton and lamb (3), pig-meat (5), poultry and eggs (1), and fish (1).

(c) Viz. dairy products (7), fruit and vegetables (5), sugar (2), tea, coffee and cocoa (3), and tobacco (2).

(d) Viz. copper (4), tin (1), lead (1), zinc (1), nickel (1), and petroleum (2).

(e) Viz. silk and artificial silk (2), linen (2), jute (1), and hemp (1).

(f) Viz. paper (2), leather (4), rubber (1), timber (4), bricks (1), stone and slate (2), and glass, china, etc. (1).

(g) The weights are as follows: Total Food—52; Coal—10; Iron and Steel—24; Other Metals and Minerals—10; Cotton—16; Wool—9; Other Textile Materials—6; Other Articles—15.

NOTES TO PART C

[1] Source: *Board of Trade Journal.*

[2] These indices are based on market prices.

C. 1930–8. 1930 = 100

| | Food and Tobacco | | | | Industrial Materials and Manufactures | | | | | | | | |
	Cereals (a)	Meat and Fish (b)	Other Foods (c)	Total	Coal	Iron and Steel	Non-ferrous Metals (d)	Cotton	Wool	Other Textiles (e)	Chemicals and Oils (f)	Miscellaneous (g)	Total Index (h)
1930	100.0	100.0	100.0	100.0	100.0	100.0	100.0	100.0	100.0	100.0	100.0	100.0	100.0
1931	82.0	82.9	97.9	88.5	102.6	92.8	80.9	79.0	81.4	78.6	89.8	86.6	87.8
1932	88.2	75.4	97.3	87.7	103.0	91.5	82.9	78.3	74.6	77.1	90.7	80.3	85.6
1933	83.3	76.9	87.2	82.9	101.5	94.3	87.2	78.7	84.9	73.1	90.3	84.4	85.7
1934	86.4	81.2	86.9	85.0	102.5	98.7	83.9	87.5	95.0	66.4	87.4	88.0	88.1
1935	89.6	80.1	89.9	86.8	102.5	100.5	86.9	86.7	90.0	69.2	91.0	86.3	89.0
1936	99.1	81.1	94.8	91.7	107.6	106.6	93.0	88.8	105.0	72.5	93.5	92.3	94.4
1937	127.0	86.4	98.7	102.2	124.9	129.6	117.4	97.7	127.5	76.3	99.4	110.2	108.7
1938	109.9	85.9	97.5	97.3	123.2	139.1	94.4	83.6	101.4	68.7	94.7	93.2	101.4

(a) Viz. wheat (8), barley (8), oats (1), maize (2), and rice (1).

(b) Viz. beef and veal (6), mutton and lamb (3), pig-meat (6), poultry and eggs (3), and fish (2).

(c) Viz. dairy products (9), fruit and vegetables (7), sugar (4), tea, coffee and cocoa (3), and tobacco (5).

(d) Viz. copper (4), lead (1), tin (1), zinc (1), and nickel and aluminum (1).

(e) Viz. silk and artificial silk (5), linen (2), jute (1), and hemp (1).

(f) Viz. chemicals, drugs, dyes, etc. (6), oils and fats (3), paints (2), and petroleum (4).

(g) Viz. paper (9), leather (5), rubber (2), timber (8), bricks (2), tiles (1), stone and slate (2), cement (1), sand, lime, etc. (1), glass (1), and china, etc. (1).

Prices 4.   The Schumpeter-Gilboy Price Indices—1661–1823

NOTES TO PART A

[1] SOURCE: Elizabeth B. Schumpeter, 'English Prices and Public Finance, 1660–1822,' *Review of Economic Statistics* (1938).
[2] The indices are based very largely on contract prices paid by institutions.
[3] All figures are for years ended Michaelmas.

Part A. 1697 = 100

	Consumers' Goods (a)	Producers' Goods (b)		Consumers' Goods (a)	Producers' Goods (b)
1661	109	96	1680	93	82
1662	113	105	1681	90	79
1663	111	97	1682	90	80
1664	105	95	1683	88	84
1665	105	101	1684	89	83
1666	101	108	1685	91	75
1667	96	112	1686	92	69
1668	96	102	1687	81	71
1669	92	92	1688	81	70
1670	93	92	1689	80	77
1671	92	97	1690	82	89
1672	89	91	1691	83	97
1673	88	96	1692	82	87
1674	94	92	1693	86	89
1675	101	89	1694	95	88
1676	96	91	1695	95	92
1677	89	87	1696	96	101
1678	90	85	1697	100	100
1679	95	86			

Year	Consumers' Goods (a)	Consumers' Goods Other Than Cereals (b)	Producers' Goods (c)	Year	Consumers' Goods (a)	Consumers' Goods Other Than Cereals (b)	Producers' Goods (c)
1696	121	112	112	1718	93	94	91
1697	122	115	109	1719	97	99	92
1698	128	119	101	1720	102	96	91
1699	132	124	102	1721	100	100	89
1700	115	107	99	1722	92	96	91
1701	100	100	100	1723	89	91	86
1702	99	99	104	1724	94	89	87
1703	94	102	104	1725	97	93	87
1704	98	95	102	1726	102	97	92
1705	89	88	102	1727	96	92	97
1706	101	100	98	1728	99	92	95
1707	88	90	95	1729	104	94	95
1708	92	89	97	1730	95	91	98
1709	107	94	100	1731	88	86	95
1710	122	104	106	1732	89	90	90
1711	135	131	109	1733	85	87	86
1712	101	98	98	1734	88	87	86
1713	97	95	96	1735	89	84	83
1714	103	95	91	1736	87	81	82
1715	104	99	86	1737	93	89	81
1716	99	96	89	1738	91	85	81
1717	95	97	90	1739	89	85	87

Prices 4. The Schumpeter-Gilboy Price Indices—1661–1823 (cont.)

	Consumers' Goods (a)	Consumers' Goods Other Than Cereals (b)	Producers' Goods (c)		Consumers' Goods (a)	Consumers' Goods Other Than Cereals (b)	Producers' Goods (c)
1740	100	85	89	1782	116	106	120
1741	108	95	97	1783	129	113	117
1742	99	97	97	1784	126	111	108
1743	94	91	91	1785	120	109	107
1744	84	86	98	1786	119	106	113
1745	85	87	81	1787	117	106	111
1746	93	94	91	1788	121	111	113
1747	90	89	86	1789	117	108	107
1748	94	95	89	1790	124	112	107
1749	96	93	91	1791	121	109	107
1750	95	91	88	1792	122	113	111
1751	90	85	85	1793	129	117	124
1752	93	87	81	1794	136	121	119
1753	90	85	81	1795	147	119	122
1754	90	85	89	1796	154	122	138
1755	92	88	91	1797	148	142	141
1756	92	89	93	1798	148	142	129
1757	109	92	94	1799	160	146	128
1758	106	94	101	1800	212	168	144
1759	100	96	101	1801	228	166	162
1760	98	97	102	1802	174	149	...
1761	94	91	101	1803	156	148	...

Year	(a)	(b)	(c)
1763	100	92	102
1764	102	94	101
1765	106	97	99
1766	107	96	99
1767	109	93	99
1768	108	92	98
1769	99	92	92
1770	100	92	94
1771	107	96	94
1772	117	103	98
1773	119	102	99
1774	116	101	98
1775	113	96	98
1776	114	102	101
1777	108	99	102
1778	117	106	104
1779	111	102	110
1780	110	106	113
1781	115	105	110
1805	187	158	..
1806	184	159	..
1807	186	159	..
1808	204	167	..
1809	212	169	..
1810	207	169	..
1811	206	183	..
1812	237	181	..
1813	243	190	..
1814	209	189	..
1815	191	190	..
1816	172	160	..
1817	189	155	..
1818	194	170	..
1819	192	174	..
1820	162	148	..
1821	139	135	..
1822	125	129	..
1823	128	121	..

(a) Viz. barley, beans, biscuits, bread, flour, oats, peas, rye, wheat, beef for salting, butter, cheese, pork, ale, beer, cider, hops, malt, pepper, raisins, sugar, tea, tallow candles, coal, broadcloth, hair, felt hats, kersey, leather backs, Brussels linen, Irish linen, blue yarn stockings.

(b) Viz. all items after wheat in footnote (a).

(c) Viz. bricks, coal, lead, pantiles, plain tiles, hemp (to 1794), leather backs (to 1793), train oil (to 1783), tallow (to 1780), lime (to 1779), glue (to 1778), and copper (to 1776).

Prices 5. Indices of Agricultural and Industrial Prices—1401–1640*

(1451–1475 = 100)

Harvest Year	Industrial Price Index (1)	Agricultural Price Index (2)	Harvest Year	Industrial Price Index (1)	Agricultural Price Index (2)
1401	103	—	1432	107	—
1402	102	—	1433	102	—
1403	118	—	1434	110	—
1404	120	—	1435	110	—
1405	124	—	1436	110	—
1406	117	—	1437	114	—
1407	117	—	1438	116	—
1408	115	—	1439	112	—
1409	109	—	1440	108	—
1410	112	—			
			1441	106	—
1411	109	—	1442	107	—
1412	114	—	1443	102	—
1413	113	—	1444	105	—
1414	109	—	1445	100	—
1415	106	—	1446	101	—
1416	103	—	1447	97	—
1417	110	—	1448	99	—
1418	113	—	1449	97	—
1419	105	—	1450	99	110
1420	98	—			
1421	101	—	1451	94	100
1422	100	—	1452	102	104
1423	103	—	1453	101	99
1424	105	—	1454	105	96
1425	105	—	1455	102	85
1426	110	—	1456	95	90
1427	110	—	1457	96	97
1428	116	—	1458	100	96
1429	112	—	1459	100	106
1430	112	—	1460	95	110
1431	112	—	1461	99	111

Harvest Year	Industrial Price Index (1)	Agricultural Price Index (2)	Harvest Year	Industrial Price Index (1)	Agricultural Price Index (2)
1462	97	98	1496	107	94
1463	99	81	1497	95	99
1464	98	117	1498	96	110
1465	99	105	1499	98	97
1466	97	94	1500	105	105
1467	96	106			
1468	99	98	1501	106	109
1469	106	108	1502	101	109
1470	96	109	1503	102	113
			1504	101	121
1471	99	105	1505	98	110
1472	103	99	1506	98	107
1473	105	99	1507	97	109
1474	103	92	1508	100	106
1475	109	96	1509	106	98
1476	110	91	1510	103	90
1477	109	100			
1478	103	109	1511	101	101
1479	98	90	1512	105	111
1480	106	94	1513	101	111
			1514	105	115
1481	99	123	1515	102	114
1482	108	142	1516	102	125
1483	102	107	1517	105	136
1484	96	108	1518	108	126
1485	103	86	1519	103	158
1486	101	106	1520	112	169
1487	106	99			
1488	107	115	1521	116	152
1489	99	96	1522	113	130
1490	102	113	1523	114	117
			1524	118	119
1491	99	102	1525	116	124
1492	97	98	1526	117	147
1493	107	92	1527	122	176
1494	103	90	1528	126	150
1495	106	100	1529	124	150

Harvest Year	Industrial Price Index (1)	Agricultural Price Index (2)	Harvest Year	Industrial Price Index (1)	Agricultural Price Index (2)
1530	116	132	1563	238	338
			1564	234	257
1531	113	156	1565	231	289
1532	114	162	1566	229	280
1533	109	143	1567	224	315
1534 ·	117	146	1568	222	328
1535	111	168	1569	231	279
1536	119	149	1570	228	289
1537	116	131			
1538	120	131	1571	234	284
1539	117	140	1572	240	332
1540	114	145	1573	239	398
			1574	239	349
1541	118	159	1575	236	333
1542	126	157	1576	247	338
1543	127	154	1577	243	340
1544	133	182	1578	239	346
1545	136	205	1579	246	354
1546	140	160	1580	244	373
1547	148	162			
1548	153	189	1581	245	378
1549	174	239	1582	239	369
1550	183	313	1583	241	346
			1584	250	326
1551	188	284	1585	258	427
1552	194	279	1586	267	491
1553	190	232	1587	266	353
1554	191	290	1588	267	362
1555	197	373	1589	266	413
1556	196	397	1590	267	507
1557	200	243			
1558	208	249	1591	264	396
1559	221	278	1592	264	348
1560	233	296	1593	267	379
			1594	277	507
1561	230	295	1595	297	528
1562	232	341	1596	306	691

Prices 5. Indices of Prices—1401–1640 (cont.)

Harvest Year	Industrial Price Index (1)	Agricultural Price Index (2)	Harvest Year	Industrial Price Index (1)	Agricultural Price Index (2)
1597	296	578	1619	307	528
1598	306	444	1620	308	486
1599	290	467			
1600	293	597	1621	308	566
			1622	320	615
1601	281	486	1623	317	569
1602	289	432	1624	304	580
1603	287	423	1625	300	630
1604	288	454	1626	311	560
1605	286	481	1627	323	513
1606	297	462	1628	331	614
1607	298	511	1629	353	661
1608	309	560	1630	346	783
1609	309	555			
1610	314	502	1631	343	619
			1632	343	685
1611	318	612	1633	341	682
1612	314	640	1634	356	780
1613	321	585	1635	340	662
1614	323	570	1636	351	714
1615	316	685	1637	354	869
1616	309	579	1638	356	663
1617	307	560	1639	352	587
1618	301	535	1640	357	630

*Reprinted from Robert A. Doughty, "Industrial Prices and Inflation in Southern England, 1401–1640," *Exploration in Economic History* **12** (1975), 177–192. Copyright © 1975 by Academic Press, Inc.

Appendix B

WHOLESALE PRICE INDICES OF THE UNITED STATES

Prices 1. Wholesale Price Indices (Warren and Pearson):
1749 to 1890

[1910–14= 100]

Year	All Commodities
1890	82
1889	81
1888	86
1887	85
1886	82
1885	85
1884	93
1883	101
1882	108
1881	103
1880	100
1879	90
1878	91
1877	106
1876	110
1875	118
1874	126
1873	133
1872	136
1871	130
1870	135
1869	151
1868	158
1867	162
1866	174
1865	185
1864	193
1863	133
1862	104
1861	89

Prices 1. Wholesale Price Indices (Warren and Pearson)—
1749–1890 (cont.)

Year	All Commodities
1860	93
1859	95
1858	93
1857	111
1856	105
1855	110
1854	108
1853	97
1852	88
1851	83
1850	84
1849	82
1848	82
1847	90
1846	83
1845	83
1844	77
1843	75
1842	82
1841	92
1840	95
1839	112
1838	110
1837	115
1836	114
1835	100
1834	90
1833	95
1832	95
1831	94
1830	91
1829	96
1828	97
1827	98
1826	99
1825	103
1824	98

Prices 1. Wholesale Prices Indices (Warren and Pearson)—
1749–1890 (cont.)

Year	All Commodities
1823	103
1822	106
1821	102
1820	106
1819	125
1818	147
1817	151
1816	151
1815	170
1814	182
1813	162
1812	131
1811	126
1810	131
1809	130
1808	115
1807	130
1806	134
1805	141
1804	126
1803	118
1802	117
1801	142
1800	129
1799	126
1798	122
1797	131
1796	146
1795	131
1794	108
1793	102
1791	85
1790	90
1789	86
1787	90
1786	90

Prices 1. Wholesale Price Indices (Warren and Pearson)—
1749–1890 (cont.)

Year	All Commodities
1785	92
1784	. . .
1783	. . .
1782	. . .
1781	216
1780	225
1779	226
1778	140
1777	123
1776	86
1775	75
1774	76
1773	84
1772	89
1771	79
1770	77
1769	77
1768	74
1767	77
1766	73
1765	72
1764	74
1763	79
1762	87
1761	77
1760	79
1759	79
1758	70
1757	65
1756	66
1755	66
1754	65
1753	65
1752	66
1751	65
1750	60
1749	68

Prices 2. Wholesale Price Indices (Bureau of Labor Statistics): 1890–1970

[1967 = 100]

Year	All Commodities
1970	110.4
1969	106.5
1968	102.5
1967	100.0
1966	99.8
1965	96.6
1964	94.7
1963	94.5
1962	94.8
1961	94.5
1960	94.9
1959	94.8
1958	94.6
1957	93.3
1956	90.7
1955	87.8
1954	87.6
1953	87.4
1952	88.6
1951	91.1
1950	81.8
1949	78.7
1948	82.8
1947	76.5
1946	62.3
1945	54.6
1944	53.6
1943	53.3
1942	50.9
1941	45.1
1940	40.5
1939	39.8
1938	40.5
1937	44.5

Prices 2. Wholesale Price Indices (BLS):
1890–1970 (cont.)

Year	All Commodities
1936	41.7
1935	41.3
1934	38.6
1933	34.0
1932	33.6
1931	37.6
1930	44.6
1929	49.1
1928	50.0
1927	49.3
1926	51.6
1925	53.3
1924	50.5
1923	51.9
1922	49.9
1921	50.3
1920	79.6
1919	71.4
1918	67.6
1917	60.6
1916	44.1
1915	35.8
1914	35.2
1913	36.0
1912	35.6
1911	33.5
1910	36.4
1909	34.9
1908	32.4
1907	33.6
1906	32.0
1905	31.0
1904	30.8
1903	30.7
1902	30.4
1901	28.5

Prices 2. Wholesale Price Indices (BLS):
1890–1970 (cont.)

Year	All Commodities
1900	28.9
1899	26.9
1898	25.0
1897	24.0
1896	23.9
1895	25.2
1894	24.7
1893	27.5
1892	26.9
1891	28.8
1890	28.9

Prices 3. Wholesale Price Indices (Bureau of Labor Statistics),
1890 to 1951

[1926 = 100]

Year	All Commodities
1951	180.4
1950	161.5
1949	155.0
1948	165.1
1947	152.1
1946	121.1
1945	105.8
1944	104.0
1943	103.1
1942	98.8
1941	87.3
1940	78.6
1939	77.1
1938	78.6
1937	86.3
1936	80.8
1935	80.0
1934	74.9
1933	65.9
1932	64.8
1931	73.0
1930	86.4
1929	95.3
1928	96.7
1927	95.4
1926	100.0
1925	103.5
1924	98.1
1923	100.6
1922	96.7
1921	97.6
1920	154.4
1919	138.6

Year	All Commodities
1918	131.3
1917	117.5
1916	85.5
1915	69.5
1914	68.1
1913	69.8
1912	69.1
1911	64.9
1910	70.4
1909	67.6
1908	62.9
1907	65.2
1906	61.8
1905	60.1
1904	59.7
1903	59.6
1902	58.9
1901	55.3
1900	56.1
1899	52.2
1898	48.5
1897	46.6
1896	46.5
1895	48.8
1894	47.9
1893	53.4
1892	52.2
1891	55.8
1890	56.2

Appendix C

THE INDEX OF WORLD PRODUCTION OF GOLD*

1493–1972

[1930 = 100.0]

Year	Index	Year	Index	Year	Index
1493	.9	1524	1.1	1555	1.3
1494	.9	1525	1.1	1556	1.3
1495	.9	1526	1.1	1557	1.3
1496	.9	1527	1.1	1558	1.3
1497	.9	1528	1.1	1559	1.3
1498	,9	1529	1.1		
1499	.9			1560	1.3
		1530	1.1	1561	1.1
1500	.9	1531	1.1	1562	1.1
1501	.9	1532	1.1	1563	1.1
1502	.9	1533	1.1	1564	1.1
1503	.9	1534	1.1	1565	1.1
1504	.9	1535	1.1	1566	1.1
1505	.9	1536	1.1	1567	1.1
1506	.9	1537	1.1	1568	1.1
1507	.9	1538	1.1	1569	1.1
1508	.9	1539	1.1		
1509	.9			1570	1.1
		1540	1.1	1571	1.1
1510	.9	1541	1.1	1572	1.1
1511	.9	1542	1.1	1573	1.1
1512	.9	1543	1.1	1574	1.1
1513	.9	1544	1.1	1575	1.1
1514	.9	1545	1.3	1576	1.1
1515	.9	1546	1.3	1577	1.1
1516	.9	1547	1.3	1578	1.1
1517	.9	1548	1.3	1579	1.1
1518	.9	1549	1.3		
1519	.9			1580	1.1
		1550	1.3	1582	1.1
1520	.9	1551	1.3	1581	1.1
1521	1.1	1552	1.3	1583	1.1
1522	1.1	1553	1.3	1584	1.1
1523	1.1	1554	1.3		

221

Year	Index	Year	Index	Year	Index
1585	1.1	1622	1.3	1660	1.4
1586	1.1	1623	1.3	1661	1.4
1587	1.1	1624	1.3	1662	1.4
1588	1.1	1625	1.3	1663	1.4
1589	1.1	1626	1.3	1664	1.4
		1627	1.3	1665	1.4
1590	1.1	1628	1.3	1666	1.4
1591	1.1	1629	1.3	1667	1.4
1592	1.1			1668	1.4
1593	1.1	1630	1.3	1669	1.4
1594	1.1	1631	1.3		
1595	1.1	1632	1.3	1670	1.4
1596	1.1	1633	1.3	1671	1.4
1597	1.1	1634	1.3	1672	1.4
1598	1.1	1635	1.3	1673	1.4
1599	1.1	1636	1.3	1674	1.4
		1637	1.3	1675	1.4
1600	1.1	1638	1.3	1676	1.4
1601	1.3	1639	1.3	1677	1.4
1602	1.3			1678	1.4
1603	1.3	1640	1.3	1679	1.4
1604	1.3	1641	1.4		
1605	1.3	1642	1.4	1680	1.4
1606	1.3	1643	1.4	1681	1.7
1607	1.3	1644	1.4	1682	1.7
1608	1.3	1645	1.4	1683	1.7
1609	1.3	1646	1.4	1684	1.7
		1647	1.4	1685	1.7
1610	1.3	1648	1.4	1686	1.7
1611	1.3	1649	1.4	1687	1.7
1612	1.3			1688	1.7
1613	1.3	1650	1.4	1689	1.7
1614	1.3	1651	1.4		
1615	1.3	1652	1.4	1690	1.7
1616	1.3	1653	1.4	1691	1.7
1617	1.3	1654	1.4	1692	1.7
1618	1.3	1655	1.4	1693	1.7
1619	1.3	1656	1.4	1694	1.7
		1657	1.4	1695	1.7
1620	1.3	1658	1.4	1696	1.7
1621	1.3	1659	1.4	1697	1.7

Year	Index	Year	Index	Year	Index
1698	1.7	1735	2.9	1772	3.2
1699	1.7	1736	2.9	1773	3.2
		1737	2.9	1774	3.2
1700	1.7	1738	2.9	1775	3.2
1701	2.0	1739	2.9	1776	3.2
1702	2.0			1777	3.2
1703	2.0	1740	2.9	1778	3.2
1704	2.0	1741	3.8	1779	3.2
1705	2.0	1742	3.8		
1706	2.0	1743	3.8	1780	3.2
1707	2.0	1744	3.8	1781	2.7
1708	2.0	1745	3.8	1782	2.7
1709	2.0	1746	3.8	1783	2.7
		1747	3.8	1784	2.7
1710	2.0	1748	3.8	1785	2.7
1711	2.0	1749	3.8	1786	2.7
1712	2.0			1787	2.7
1713	2.0	1750	3.8	1788	2.7
1714	2.0	1751	3.8	1789	2.7
1715	2.0	1752	3.8		
1716	2.0	1753	3.8	1790	2.7
1717	2.0	1754	3.8	1791	2.7
1718	2.0	1755	3.8	1792	2.7
1719	2.0	1756	3.8	1793	2.7
		1757	3.8	1794	2.7
1720	2.0	1758	3.8	1795	2.7
1721	2.9	1759	3.8	1796	2.7
1722	2.9			1797	2.7
1723	2.9	1760	3.8	1798	2.7
1724	2.9	1761	3.2	1799	2.7
1725	2.9	1762	3.2		
1726	2.9	1763	3.2	1800	2.7
1727	2.9	1764	3.2	1801	2.7
1728	2.9	1765	3.2	1802	2.7
1729	2.9	1766	3.2	1803	2.7
		1767	3.2	1804	2.7
1730	2.9	1768	3.2	1805	2.7
1731	2.9	1769	3.2	1806	2.7
1732	2.9			1807	2.7
1733	2.9	1770	3.2	1808	2.7
1734	2.9	1771	3.2	1809	2.7

Appendix C (*continued*)

Year	Index	Year	Index	Year	Index
1810	2.7	1848	8.5	1885	24.0
1811	1.8	1849	8.5	1886	24.2
1812	1.8			1887	24.6
1813	1.8	1850	8.5	1888	25.6
1814	1.8	1851	19.4	1889	28.7
1815	1.8	1852	30.0		
1816	1.8	1853	35.1	1890	27.6
1817	1.8	1854	28.8	1891	30.3
1818	1.8	1855	30.5	1892	34.1
1819	1.8	1856	33.4	1893	36.6
		1857	30.1	1894	42.1
1820	1.8	1858	28.2	1895	46.2
1821	2.2	1859	28.2	1896	47.0
1822	2.2			1897	54.8
1823	2.2	1860	26.9	1898	66.1
1824	2.2	1861	25.7	1899	71.2
1825	2.2	1862	24.4		
1826	2.2	1863	24.2	1900	59.1
1827	2.2	1864	25.5	1901	61.0
1828	2.2	1865	27.2	1902	68.9
1829	2.2	1866	27.4	1903	76.1
		1867	25.8	1904	80.7
1830	2.2	1868	24.8	1905	88.3
1831	3.1	1869	24.0	1906	93.5
1832	3.1			1907	95.9
1833	3.1	1870	24.1	1908	102.9
1834	3.1	1871	28.7	1909	105.4
1835	3.1	1872	27.3		
1836	3.1	1873	26.7	1910	105.7
1837	3.1	1874	25.9	1911	107.3
1838	3.1	1875	25.7	1912	108.2
1839	3.1	1876	25.5	1913	110.1
		1877	26.9	1914	104.8
1840	3.1	1878	24.9	1915	109.7
1841	8.5	1879	24.2	1916	104.6
1842	8.5			1917	98.6
1843	8.5	1880	25.0	1918	88.8
1844	8.5	1881	23.9	1919	82.6
1845	8.5	1882	23.2		
1846	8.5	1883	23.3	1920	77.4
1847	8.5	1884	23.5	1921	76.7

Year	Index	Year	Index	Year	Index
1922	75.4	1940	196.6	1958	153.7
1923	88.0	1941	188.9	1959	164.8
1924	92.4	1942	165.3		
1925	93.0	1943	127.9		
1926	92.9	1944	115.0	1960	172.3
1927	93.3	1945	110.6	1961	177.7
1928	93.1	1946	112.1	1962	190.1
1929	95.5	1947	113.0	1963	202.0
		1948	116.3	1964	208.7
1930	100.0	1949	119.5	1965	213.4
1931	107.5			1966	213.5
1932	116.8	1950	123.6	1967	209.0
1933	121.7	1951	121.0	1968	209.2
1934	131.1	1952	124.5	1969	209.2
1935	142.0	1953	124.0		
1936	159.2	1954	131.2		
1937	168.0	1955	137.5	1970	215.0
1938	179.7	1956	143.3	1971	209.2
1939	187.5	1957	149.0	1972	213.4

*This index reflects the best estimates the author can make of the worldwide production of gold for the years in question. Principal sources used are J. Laurence Laughlin, "Gold and Prices, 1890–1907," *Journal of Political Economy,* May 1909 for the period 1493–1850; *The Statist, Journal of the Royal Statistical Society* for the period 1851–1949; *International Financial Statistics,* relevant volumes, International Monetary Fund for the period 1950–1972. The *Minerals Year Book,* U.S. Department of the Interior, has also been useful.

Sources and Computations of Gold Prices
in England

I. Sources

1560-1716	dependent on Mint prices
1717-1759	dependent on Bank of England buying prices
1760-1829	prices compiled by John White, Cashier of the Bank of the United States, as Senate Executive Document No. 58, Forty-fifth Congress, Third Session. Also found in Report of Proceedings of International Monetary Conference in Paris, 1878, p. 647
1830-1869	dependent on Bank of England buying prices
1870-1932	prices compiled by I. Shrigley, The Price of Gold, P. S. King & Son Ltd., 1935
1933-1939	dependent on quarterly memoranda of the Royal Economic Society
1940-1967	(excluding 1960) prices compiled from the London Times
1968-1976	(and 1960) prices compiled from International Financial Statistics, International Monetary Fund

II. Notes

1. 1940-1949   The September 1949 devaluation effect on the price of gold was first given effect in 1950.

2. 1950-1976   The price of gold in London in this period was reported in US dollars. Thus the index was effected by any change in the £/US\$ exchange rate.

Using 1949 as a base (i.e. Gold Price Index = 220.7, Gold Price = \$35, Exchange rate = \$4.02/£1) the index was found as follows:

$$i^{th} \text{ year Gold Price Index} = 220.7 \left(\frac{\$4.02}{i^{th} \text{ year exchange rate}} \right) \left(\frac{i^{th} \text{ year \$ gold price}}{\$35} \right)$$

$$\text{OR} = (220.7) \left(\frac{\$4.02}{\$35} \right) \left(\frac{i^{th} \text{ year \$ gold price}}{i^{th} \text{ year exchange rate}} \right)$$

3. 1950-1959   Gold price was taken as $35.15 since the price
                fluctuated between $35.05 and $35.25
                Exchange rate was US$2.80 = £1

4. 1960   Gold price increased to $35.25 due to speculative
                activity in the market
                Exchange rate was US$2.80 = £1

5. 1961-1967   As for 1950-1959
                Note: The November 1967 devaluation was ignored
                       until 1968

6. 1968-1970,   Gold price, current market price as reported in
      1972   IMF International Financial Statistics
                Exchange rate US$2.40 = £1

7. 1971   Gold price, as in 1968-1970, 1972
                Exchange rate taken as US$2.55 = £1. This average
                rate prevailed during the monetary crises in 1971
                when the US dollar was devalued.

8. 1973-1976   The price of gold was found by taking the average
                of the end of quarter figures reported by the IMF
                and dividing by the current exchange rate.

9. 1960, 1968- The price of gold and the exchange rate were found
      1976   in the International Financial Statistics published
                by the International Monetary Fund.

10.   The yearly average price of gold in 1968 was com-
                puted using the January 1968 and February 1968
                price of gold (each 1/11 of the weight) and the II,
                III, IV quarter price of gold (each 3/11's of the
                weight). March 1968 was not included since the
                London Gold Market was closed for part of that month.

11.   The yearly average price of gold in 1969 was compu-
                ted from the quarterly prices reported.

12.   For 1960, 1970-1972, the price of gold was computed
                from the monthly prices reported.

13.   For 1973-1976 the price of gold was computed from
                the quarterly prices reported.

Index

It was not thought necessary to separate the English and American indexes or to identify each item by a national reference. All page numbers before 135 belong to the English Experience, all those after to the American.

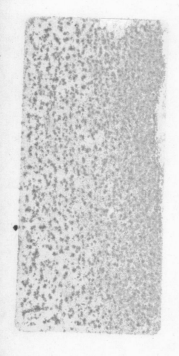